Keeping Heidi Close

Becoming Available to My Orb-Angel

Cindy Mitchell Perkins
and
Heidi Louise Tobiason

Leaning Rock Press

Leaning Rock Press
Gales Ferry, CT 06335
leaningrockpress@gmail.com
www.leaningrockpress.com

Copyeditor: Florence Kilgo

978-1-960596-16-1, Hardcover
978-1-960596-17-8, Softcover

Library of Congress Control Number: 2024904672

Publisher's Cataloging-in-Publication Data
(Prepared by Cassidy Cataloguing's PCIP Service)

Names:	Perkins, Cindy Mitchell, author.	Tobiason, Heidi Louise, author.
Title:	Keeping Heidi close : becoming available to my orb-angel / Cindy Mitchell Perkins and Heidi Louise Tobiason.
Description:	Gales Ferry, CT : Leaning Rock Press, [2024]	Includes bibliographical references and index.
Identifiers:	ISBN: 978-1-960596-16-1 (hardcover)	978-1-960596-17-8 (softcover)	LCCN: 2024904672
Subjects:	LCSH: Perkins, Cindy Mitchell--Family.	Parental grief.	Children--Death--Psychological aspects.	Loss (Psychology)	Grief--Religious aspects--Christianity.	Guilt.	Traffic accidents.	BISAC: PSYCHOLOGY / Grief & Loss.	FAMILY & RELATIONSHIPS / Death, Grief, Bereavement.	RELIGION / Christian Living / Death, Grief, Bereavement.
Classification:	LCC: BF575.G7 P47 2024	DDC: 155.937085--dc23

Printed in the United States of America

Dedication

This book is dedicated to my Mom, Bobbie, who now sits with Heidi, smiling, as I receive messages from both of them to support the publication of this book. Mom taught me, by example, to pay attention to any and all communication from loved ones who had died. She was a true intuitive before many of us understood what that meant. She bravely shared messages from loved ones to audiences made up of friends, family, and strangers, some of whom made fun of her. This did not stop her. I long for the conversations that I am now ready to have with you, Mom.

Mom's courageous sharing of spiritual messages from loved ones and her belief in life beyond this earthly realm has given me the confidence to trust my experiences and have helped bring this book forward in the hope that it may help other parents.

Mom's honesty, faith, and vulnerability have led me to my wonderful new relationship with my Orb-Angel Heidi.

I love you and thank you Mom.

Disclaimer

The experiences in this book represent my perspective on everything that happened. It is my intent to tell this story from my perspective and not anyone else's.

MORE PRAISE FOR *Keeping Heidi Close*

"I am struck by the honesty and vulnerability that Cindy has put forth in this book about her journey since her daughter, Heidi, died in 1994. She is not afraid to talk about the hardest feelings and at the same time is able to bring joy and hope forward as she has walked through the years. Cindy's experiences beg the question: Why would we want to limit God's ways of walking with us through our lives?" - *Rev. Don Hayn, Retired ELCA.*

"It seems strange to refer to a book about a mother losing her daughter from this world as beautiful but that's the word that comes to mind. The combination of journal entries, poetry and drawings from those early days along with her hindsight reflections are layered together so beautifully. It's such a raw look at the complexity of grief and the many ways we try to make sense of losses that are incomprehensible."- *Renee Cunningham, Owner of Oliver & Friends Bookshop.*

"One does not have to be a grieving parent to read this beautiful book. It brings readers hope, as well as a myriad of choices to learn to cope, not only with grief, but with life" - *Patricia Ferrara Fuchs, MS Ed Counseling, Artist, Poet/Writer.*

"This book is such a labor of love. I truly can't believe it will be 30 years since dear Heidi left, and now is watching over us. Author, teacher, advocate, mother, sister, friend: You are the whole package. - *Deede Russell Baiti, Grieving Grandmother.*

"This is a powerful message that you're bravely putting out there with Heidi, and really important. I was sitting here all teary this morning." - *Jenn Shaffer, Artist.*

"Thank you Cindy and Heidi for sharing your tender story of the deepest love between mom and daughter, here and there. Your combined presence of grace nurtures our Souls to look for and to find peace amongst the most painful of life's experiences." - *M. B. Russell RN, Intuitive Consultant, Reiki Master/Teacher, CranioSacral Practitioner.*

"In reading the pages of this book, I'm struck by the gift we receive while reading these pages which is totally dependent on vulnerability. We feel this mom's honest assessment of pain, loss and ongoing questions ... we wrestle with the invisibility of a rulebook for how to properly process whatever pain happens in us ... and we come to see that another's journey is nearly incomprehensible. Nearly. Perkins reaches a hand and a heart — dripping with her own vulnerability — so that we can all experience a morsel of wonder that has immeasurable depth. What a gift!" - *Knute Ogren, Director of Development & Communications, Intern Coordinator Calumet Outdoor Ministries, Ossipee, NH.*

Table of Contents

Introduction

"Grief is not linear." That is something I often tell people. Grief is a double helix. It is so tight and wrenching sometimes, and other times you can move from the dark center of your grief to breathe and live, without feeling the depth of your pain. I know this to be true from experience, and yet, I tried to force this book's content to be linear. How can a book about grief and loss be linear if grief itself is not? I had originally named the book "Love, Loss, and Hope." In that way, I tried to put everything into three parts, as if I could. In the final version of this book, you will find parts of my narrative cycle back again in my journal or my story, showing the ways in which grief is not a linear progression.

My therapist, Stephanie, would often say, "as if . . ." in such a profound way that I would stop and listen to what I was saying at a deeper level. For example, I would say it was my job to keep my children safe, or I should have kept them safe. . . . Her response, "as if . . .," would lead me to understand that I could not protect my children from everything, no matter how hard I tried and how much I wanted to. Initially, my search, I came to learn, was more about trying to change what had happened. If I could find the why, then I could go back in time and the outcome would be different. As if . . . I could change the outcome. . . .

Of course, I kept searching and learned that we are not in control of everything, even though we want to be and wish, oh, how we wish, to be in control, especially of keeping our precious children safe.

My message in this book is that some things just are and we don't get to understand the why that we so want the answer to. Maybe there are reasons so much bigger than us that we cannot grasp or explain. It doesn't mean that we don't keep searching. Of course, we do. Some

1

things we just know. Is learning to trust what we already know in our hearts part of our journey? Yes, I say, . . . yes. Certainly, this has been true for me. Daring to look into my own heart has brought every feeling imaginable and yet also continues to ultimately bring me peace. Sometimes during my search, I found that I would argue with the answer I knew to be true because I did not want that to be the answer. I had to learn to trust my own heart and my own truth.

Some parts of your journey will stretch your logical left brain along the way, as happened to me. I hope you will learn, as I did, that stretching the mind and heart and being open to new experiences is a comforting part of healing.

I hope the narrative of my experience can be helpful to you. If the order does not work for you, you might scramble it up and read it in the way you need to.

How to Read This Book

There are three voices in this book. I chose to identify them so you could distinguish between my raw unedited journals and my reflective process, as I have moved through these many years since 1994. They are distinguished by different fonts:

1. *My voice from actual journals, unchanged from when they were written.(italics)*

2. My reflections on my journal entries and my narrative in this book. (regular print)

3. Heidi's voice, because she did take over, to correct me or add things from time to time, which came through as thoughts and feel ings I could not ignore. This also includes a writing of hers from before June 10, 1994.

Losing My Child Is
(Written in 1994)

Losing my child is
waking up in agony every morning
running on a treadmill
getting nowhere in slow motion
pain that overwhelms me when I see it in others
pain that I don't want to believe I have.

Searching for joy
so I don't have to feel the pain
finding out that even joy won't take it away
guilt that the joy is there

Fear
of losing another loved one
of being buried in grief
not being able to get up one day
that the fight to keep going will beat me
of stopping and being alone with
my grief and pain.

Fear freezing over me
thinking about any movement in my life
feels like moving mountains
wanting to say that I can't do anything today
wanting to stop and fall apart.

Wanting not to have to think about anything or anyone else
not wanting to take care of anyone else's feelings
wanting to fall into my pain and sit there
AND
it terrifies me at the same time . . .
I don't want my pain to hurt the people I love.

Keeping Heidi Close

I feel so heavy and so sad
I feel surrounded and fenced in
I know there are things out there that would make me happy
and even be fun
solutions to problems that seem unbearable
but . . . I can't break the fence down
it is built high and strong.

Anguish,
loud, heavy sobbing
birthing screams,
chills in the night
two people? There?
with Heidi?
real?

pictures in my head
make them go away
friends holding me together
as I cry from my soul
hands touching as I writhe
in the pain of my heart
fogginess
surgery.

planning my child's funeral
surreal
visiting hours
funeral Service
many people
this can't be real.

waking up each morning
moment of hope that it was a dream
reality hits
again . . . and again.

Invitation

Dear Grieving Parent,

Dear Moms and Dads who have had to join this "club." This "club" no one imagines that they will EVER join. My heart aches every time I hear of another child lost, no matter the age. We parents are just not supposed to outlive our children. It's not the way it is SUPPOSED to be. We are supposed to somehow control that. WE are supposed to keep our children safe from all harm. We are conditioned to believe the fantasy that we have that kind of control. I did everything I thought I was supposed to: held their little heads, used car seats, buckled seat belts, drove safe cars, preached about bike helmets, took them to swimming lessons, worried about their every fall, every bump, hovered over fevers and coughs, went to the doctor, on and on. If only . . . .

The death of a child shakes you to your core. For me, everything I thought I knew to be true was tossed up in the air, came down in completely new patterns, much like a puzzle that I had to put back together, but that now had a new design with no edges, no recognizable patterns, and for which I had no picture, to see how it was going to look.

This book recounts my journey. Over the last twenty-nine years and beyond, I have written, drawn, taken photos, talked to friends, strangers, and my therapist. I have expressed myself in every style imaginable in order to process feelings and thoughts for myself, and ultimately for anyone who might find it helpful. The journey evolved as I have evolved. I have become a very different person from the one I was before June 10, 1994. I now savor every moment of my life. I laugh, love, and cry more quickly and am stronger than before. I am short on patience with myself when I sweat the small stuff. I am keenly aware that this may be my moment and I need to make the most of it. I am passionate about my life's work helping children and their parents.

To show my progression, I include unedited journal entries and commentary expressing responses to some of those and then the narrative of my story of the years. I also detail parts of my childhood that are pertinent to my journey of grief, including my spiritual quest.

Growing up, I lived with my mother's grief. She lost her dear brother during World War II, when she was in high school. His body was never found. She also lost a child, my brother. My big brother Douglas lived an hour. In many ways, I lived in the shadow of those people. My mother searched for answers her whole life. She often would speak very openly of messages and communications with them and with other loved ones who had died. Within her family she was often laughed at for this serious spiritual connection that she felt and shared. I grew up believing my mother but not daring to say so out loud, because I did not want to be made fun of.

My journey has taken me down similar paths. As I started to experience connections to my daughter, through hearing and seeing her, I did not dare to believe they were true, yet I knew they were. I could quickly convince myself I just wanted them to be true, partly because I did not want anyone to laugh at me. I am fortunate that my strong-willed daughter (even after she died) would not give up on me. I am fortunate to have friends who listened and walked patiently with me on this journey. I came kicking and screaming to my belief and a new strong spiritual connection with Heidi. I now realize that sometimes I thought it would be easier to not pay attention. That has not turned out to be true, but I had to be ready to listen.

My experience at the moment of her death was the first of many, over the years, undeniable episodes of contact with Heidi after the accident. My strongest memory is of seeing her walk hand and hand with two very loved people who had both died previously. That message and the many I have received and learned to pay attention to since then are described later in this book.

I was in graduate school in 1994. Heidi was very proud of me being in school. I was studying clinical psychology. I was on a track to understand grief and trauma. Very grounded grief work, incorporating my grief and my spiritual experiences, became part of my work. I was in a small, close group of fifteen in grad school so, as I grieved, so did my classmates. As I walked this path of learning, so did they. I will always be indebted to them for their strong support during that time, including the day early on when they ran ahead, during a Harvard Square lunch break, to the balloon guy who made me a silly balloon hat and got me to laugh.

This book is written and shared in hopes that some part of it may speak to you. It is my wish that it may help you or your loved ones on this journey on which no one expects to embark. It is not my intent to say I know it all or I know how to do this. Everyone has to figure out their own journey. Though a common thread unites us, I do not know your grief, as no one else knows mine. We all are individuals, so of course there is no guidebook for how to grieve the loss of our precious children. They are their own sweet souls we were trusted to care for as long as they were here. I know for me, physically seeing other moms who had lost a child, gave me strength to keep going. Reading what others had so bravely shared boosted me on days when I wasn't sure I could get through this. Some parts of their journeys resonated, while others did not.

On June 10, 1994, we were singing on our way to swimming lessons. Abruptly, the music stopped when a truck driver fell asleep and ran his vehicle into the back of my child-filled van at a toll booth. My Daughter, Heidi, eleven at the time, died instantly. My six-year-old son, Hans, ended up with stitches in his forehead and his innocence lost and child-hood altered forever. Heidi's friend Rebecca, eleven, had bumps, bruises and her innocence also stolen in that instant. All three children had trusted adults, and me specifically, to keep them safe. All three children, who were my responsibility to bring safely to their swimming lessons, had their lives dramatically altered. As much as I intellectually know that it was an accident and not my "fault," as a parent some part of me always will feel responsible. Little did I know or understand on that day how this trauma and loss would impact the rest of the young lives of the two surviving children.

What is in this book is not what I had planned to write when I first sat down to describe who Heidi was. I had heard of people who described their fingers typing but, someone else (not of this plane) actually doing the creating. Then, it happened to me.

Sometimes it's as if she pushes me over and takes over the keyboard. The section in script below is the result of one of those times (I warned you earlier that my logical left brain was pushed). I was physically putting my fingers to the keyboard but I did not write or think these words. I did not change the font. When I reread the passage, I cried hard tears and smiled at the same time. There was no question for me that Heidi's voice was in these words. My only explanation, though not from my logical brain, is that Heidi formulated that part. I cannot explain that to you. I just know deep in my being that I did not write these words but Heidi somehow did. This is what I mean when I state that Heidi and I have written this book. That is as much who Heidi was and still is as any of the other descriptions found here.

Twelve years after the day she took over my keyboard, I sat again to write the introduction for this book and attempted to write a letter from her perspective. It sounded familiar to me as I was typing. I (or she), I realized later, had written almost the same letter again twelve years later. The repeated experience of her taking over the keyboard brought tears and a smile. She still makes me smile even when I don't want to. What follows is Heidi's introduction written when she took over my keyboard.

Hi Folks,

My name is Heidi. A long time ago, my mom and I decided we were going to write a book together. This book was not what we had in mind.

We were thinking of a cute little picture book and then maybe a chapter book. We may still do that, but now this book is more important. We want to help other people along this journey that my mom and I have been on called Life.

I wasn't always Heidi. I was going to be Jennifer or Sven until the night of March 8, 1983, when after a day of full induced labor the doctors offered my mom dinner and rest and a fresh start on March 9th or keep going and I would be born sometime in the night. She decided to wait one more day to meet me. Her and my dad talked that night and my dad surprised my mom by saying, " you know, I've decided I like that Heidi name after all". This was the name my mom loved from the movie Heidi - and so Heidi I became. They joked that I didn't want to be Jennifer or Sven so didn't come out till they had the right name. No joke - Though Jennifer is a perfectly wonderful name - it wasn't my name. Louise was a given as that was after my Beloved Aunt Louise (Dad's sister who died when I was in second grade).

Let's go back so you know my whole story. My mom Cindy and my dad David had been waiting for 5 years for me. They had tried and tried to have a child and now Here I am! They were so excited. And I can't even tell you how excited my Mom's mom, Bobbie, was. She handed out stork napkins and paper plates when my parents got engaged and invited Dad's parents - my Far-far and Far-mor for lunch in 1974!!!! She was hoping I was not long behind the wedding. Well, that didn't happen! I took my time. I knew I had to have the right parents so I was out there looking and one day I found Cindy and Dave! Mom and Dad. Fast forward to March 9, 1983.

I guess I'll let mom tell the story from here, after all, "WE" are writing this book. I may have to step in from time to time if she gets something wrong.

Love,
Heidi

But I was not the only one dealing with the tragedy. My six-year-old, Heidi's friend Rebecca, her family, and David (Heidi and Hans's dad) were also left with the trauma of that day. Their journeys had a profound effect on me, too. Most especially, my sweet, hurting, loving Hans is why I got up for, so many mornings. I wanted so to be there for him. That child is now a grown man and carries that day in his heart and soul too. Like me, he has to walk his grieving path now. As much as I have always wanted to carry his load too, I couldn't then and can't now. I'm there for him when he reaches out and trust his strong heart and soul to pick him up. I hope my journey has modeled some paths for him that might help. I am also painfully aware that I made mistakes along the way, as all of us parents do. It seems that we are human even in parenting—the most important job in our lives.

My faith got me up and knocked me down as I held on, pushed away, came back, questioned, and learned that I have to believe and I do believe. I have to believe there is a bigger reason that I don't get to understand. I don't believe in coincidences anymore. I have been shown differently. That's what has gotten me twenty-nine and more years along this road.

Over time, my feelings have not usually been as raw and painful as they were early on, and yet, some days, some years are still harder than others. The unexpected jar of a feeling deep inside, a pain or a beautiful memory can bring a smile, a tear, laughter, or a crying jag. They are all part of me and my journey that I share with you so that, if it resonates with you, you may find hope. I do believe I have been shown these experiences not just to help me but to give hope to others. If you are one of those people who can find a thread or a lifeline to hold onto through my sharing, then, embrace what helps and know that we feel honored to have extended a hand in your time of most need.

Lovingly,
Cindy and Heidi

Heidi Energy
by Mom

Heidi. . . .
Slow down. . . .
I can't understand what you are saying. . . .
You are talking too fast. . . .
With your mouth full of a palate expander
it became even harder to decipher
those important messages you
had to deliver.

You had hardly taken a breath
since that first word uttered back
during those miraculous
vocabulary developing days. . . .
You had a lifetime of things to say. . . .
And only eleven years to say them all. . . .
Eleven years was to be your lifetime. . . .
You lived it as if you knew. . . .

Slowing down was not to happen. . . .
Questions came so fast
that no one could answer them all. . . .
We tried . . . your dad and I. . . .
Answers . . .
you had those too.

You so wanted to teach your brother . . .
your cousins and friends . . .
all your vast knowledge. . . .
Let's play school!

Teacher role was always yours. . . .
Why would it be any different?
Why would anyone question that?
Even when I—your mom—was the real teacher
at our little private school
you believed in your heart you were the teacher.

Although you left us in your physical way . . .
you still are the teacher.
As I awaken every day to your new presence,
(a presence I am sure of)
that is both same and
different,
I realize you are still the teacher.

You are my teacher about life here . . .
about the many
opportunities for
growing and learning
in this lifetime . . .
AND . . .
every day I am grateful
for your insistence
that
I pay attention.

Cindy Mitchell Perkins

Heidi with her Mom and Dad
A few days after birth - 1983

Heidi Louise Tobiason

In order to know my grief and walk along with me on this journey, you should meet Heidi. I wish you to know who she is, so that you know and feel my love and hers. I have included an introduction to Heidi in her first eleven years, so that you can fully appreciate her continued presence in the minds and hearts of those who knew her. I know that, to this day, a grieving parent sharing a favorite story of their child is still heartwarming and healing for me. Sharing and hearing stories of our children is a precious gift of healing that reaches both the telling parent and the listening parent. I introduce you now to Heidi, my daughter.

Heidi rushes in the door—the sliding door slams so hard I think it will break. The trumpet drops to the floor with a crash. She is talking so fast, I can hardly understand her. The retainer in her mouth doesn't help. "Heidi, slow down. I can't understand you. Take a breath. What has happened?"

"Mr. L'Heureux said I can only ask six questions a day. He gave me six cards and said that is all the questions I could ask every day." (By now, she is sobbing).

"Mom, (Gasp) Mom. What if I have seven questions that I really need to know? Or eight or ten? It's not fair. I can't do that. Why is he being so mean?"

As she paces around our living room, I try to respond while understanding his goal—my mantra often was, "Heidi, do you already know the answer to that question?" "Honey, maybe Mr. L'Heureux is trying to help you. Maybe he just wants you to think about whether you already know the answer." Of course, that is not helpful in that moment. She just cries harder.

Many "BUT MOM's" later and then some hugs, I am finally able to be more empathetic to her instead of immediately trying to help her understand her teacher.

She so needed me to hear and understand her fear. Heidi was fully sincere and passionate about anything she did. We later agree she could ask Mr. L'Heureaux about what happened if she had that very important question still after her six questions were used up. Having that option calmed her and she returned to class as enthusiastic as ever.

That was Heidi, full of curiosity, high energy, and needing answers immediately to all her questions. If I answered one question, she would have many more to follow. "I don't know," was simply not an acceptable response. People in our lives are there for a reason. As I write this, I have a big grin on my face realizing that my dear friend Abby is like Heidi in this way. When I try to tell her something, she often interrupts with wanting to know every detail (most of which have never occurred to me). I guess having my friend Abby is a way that a piece of Heidi stays in my life. I smile as I feel Heidi looking down today, beaming, saying, "oh, finally you get that mom?!"

Heidi's arrival into this world did not go as expected. Heidi tells most of this part better than I do previously in the section "Invitation." There had been no rush to the hospital, just a tearful walk across the street from my doctor's office to the hospital on March 7th.

We were assured that we would definitely be meeting our baby on March 9th. In the evening of March 9, we welcomed our beautiful, precious Heidi Louise Tobiason into the world as if she was sliding into home plate after a slow run around the bases. After not leaving my side for two days, her dad had left the room for a quick phone call (no cell phones then) to the grandparents and to grab something to eat fast. He no sooner had gotten out of ear shot when she decided she was coming. He almost missed her entrance, but got back just in time so she could slide into our arms.

Heidi was an easy baby, welcomed by her extended family and happy to be passed around from one loving set of arms to another. On the way home, this included a visit with her grandmother, great-grandmother and a few great-aunts who could not wait another second to hold her.

We lived by the lake then and by summer she was being passed around the many visitors who came to vacation. As an infant, she swam in the lake and spent her days lakeside.

Swimming was starting to be her passion in her fifth-grade year. On the way home from basketball practice one day, she hesitantly said, "Mom?"

"Yes," I replied.

She continued with, "I know you love basketball, but, (long pause) I really don't. Do you think I could do something else instead?" The caring way she asked was typical of her concern for others. She went on to join the swim team that winter. Ironically, she died on the way to help younger children with their swimming lessons.

Heidi learning to walk, 1983

Heidi's enthusiasm for life was contagious. She put her whole self into any celebration. Birthdays, Christmas, Saint Lucia Day, Fourth of July all had to be celebrated to their fullest. If there was a lull between official events, she would invent one and we would have a new tradition.

Her brother's birthday shortly after she died was obviously hard for everyone. We wanted it to be a birthday party to celebrate him only a short month and a half from losing his sister. It was at that party where it really hit me how much her energy drove our celebrations. The yard was filled with children playing, presents, cake, and supportive adults. Heidi's commanding voice organizing the younger children in her games and activities was missing. She would have spent weeks planning and coming up with new ideas daily. There would have been many more organized games, craft projects and singing that day, had Heidi been in charge.

You would have thought his birthday was her own. As an older sibling she anticipated his as much as hers. Driving through town the spring before she died, we passed a yard sale with ice hockey equipment. She spotted it and insisted that we go back and see if it would fit her brother for his birthday, as he loved hockey. We got that equipment on her insistence and he got his birthday present from his sister even that year. Thank goodness I listened and went back—not that I had much choice when Heidi got something in her head.

Heidi holding Hans, hours after his birth

The day he was born, she waited with my mother for us to call so they could come meet her new sibling (not knowing whether the baby was a boy or a girl). My mother later reported that not many minutes passed without her asking when they were going to go see her new baby. The precious photo with her big grin as she held him that first day shows all the love that was between them from day one.

Did they have their sibling moments? Of course, they did! Yet, when all was said and done, they adored each other. Saint Patrick's Day of 1994 there was an argument over the candy left by the leprechauns. Years later, Hans felt bad that he had been mean to his sister. In her bible I found an apology note from her to him. This mutual owning of the argument was typical of their love for each other.

She had a love/hate relationship with his ease in athletics. At eight and four years of age respectively, they were playing baseball in the yard when she came in and threw her softball glove down. "It's just not fair," she cried. "He's only four and he can hit the ball better than I can."

He followed her lead in whatever creative crazy endeavor she might suggest. She could get him to dress up as anything, be in a play with neighbors and cousins, or go on the many adventures of the imagination that she led. When her dad and I returned from a trip to Tortola, an Island in the British Virgin Islands, with bags of gifts for Heidi and Hans, Heidi decided that they both would put on all the clothes we got them, one on top of the other. This translated into many layers of bathing suits, t-shirts, dresses, and hats. This memory, I will always hold dearly.

Heidi's passion for her brother extended to her love of friends and cousins. In the summer of '93, Heidi was anxiously waiting for her "Bobbsey Twin" friend Andy to arrive at Camp Calumet so that they could go to resident camp for their treasured two weeks of camp. Her non-stop "when will they get here? Why aren't they here yet?" began the minute she woke that morning and continued until they, at long last, pulled into the parking lot. The two of them with outstretched arms running toward each other for that long-awaited hug was typical of how she so fully embraced her friends.

She got several friends from home to join her at Camp Calumet. I think she invited everyone she knew. She loved it there and wanted everyone to experience the joy she felt when there.

I have said that Heidi lives on. I hope meeting her in her first eleven years helps you also embrace who she has been to me since then. What she has offered to me and to many who knew her is there for the taking if one is open to listening and watching. That part is up to each of us. We will all take what we need at any given moment in our lives. Each of us hears and listens to what resonates for us.

I have learned from her through these many years. That learning had begun before she was born. I learned to be patient and wait. I wanted a child so badly. I watched friends and relatives have their children and I waited. Her dad and I had all but given up on a birth child when she showed up. She astounded me and pushed my learning from her first moment in my womb to even now, these many years later.

My precious first child, Heidi Louise Tobiason. You were your own person from day one. You always knew what you wanted and were determined to get it. You challenged me, pushed me, taught me, and got me to grow in ways that I never imagined. You got me to do things that I resisted while stretching me and getting me to reach for new horizons.

AND you have continued to do so in new ways since June 10, 1994. You're still here and very much in my life and my decisions and continuing to push and challenge me. I have had to look at things I wasn't sure I wanted to. Your guidance has helped me understand things differently and believe in so much. You are persistent as always. We had a plan to write a book. Over the years, I have written, journaled, drawn, and talked about this book. I have felt your presence all along. I will have a thought out of the blue that I need to write down. I will feel a nudge about something that needs to be in this book and know it's coming from you. I will wake in the morning sensing your presence and feel the need to write something down. It has taken me over twenty years to finally get determined and settle into my writing group, Calliope, and twenty-nine to be ready to reach out and look into getting it published. I hear you saying with a beautiful smile, "FINALLY." Look, you're still here writing this book with me.

Heidi, I have learned so much from you in the years since you left us so quickly in 1994. Our hearts were broken. We did not know how to go on. Me, your dad, your brother, family, and friends were all devastated. We could not imagine a world without you in it. Little did I know that though you were not to be here in the way I wanted, you were to be here guiding us every day. I believe that my learning to pay attention has taken a lot of persistence on your part. You made sure I had the right people in my life to help me on this journey. I pay attention more quickly now than I did at first.

In the beginning my pain was so great, I had to grieve the plans, the hopes and dreams for you and for our family, so that I could accept that you are still here and I, the one who I thought was in charge, actually had no control at all.

I tried desperately to create stories that changed reality. If only . . . I had taken a different road. If only . . . we had chosen a different car. . . On and on the variations went but reality did not change. You were gone and we had to go on. My planned story was not to be.

Heidi at one of her most favorite places: Storyland, 1986

HLT

You were such a happy child.
You brought such joy . . .
so easy going . . .
easy to please.

You rolled through the baby years . . .
sleeping nights . . .
napping . . .
smiling and cooing for everyone.
Happily being passed from one loving
family member or friend to another.

You then slid into the toddler years . . .
laughing
making friends . . .
always happy to do whatever we did.
Bedtime was hard. . . .
You didn't want to stop.

A New Brother !!
The Joy and Love in
your eyes as you held him
for the first time.
The pride as he became his own person . . .
love of being best friends . . .
happy to spend days at home . . .
creating your own adventures.

Elementary school. . . .
New joys. . . .
Lots of new friends. . . .
Activities like skating . . .
dancing. . . Brownies. . . .
Overnight Camp at
Camp Calumet.

On to Middle School. . . .
Trumpeting. . . . Math Team, Swim Team.
You were becoming a young lady
studying with a seriousness I never had.
I learned from you . . .
I am still learning from you!
Thank You

Mom

Her dad's cousin, Wayne Tobiason, captured her spirit and their special relationship (typical of so many others in her short life) beautifully in his "Buffalo and Giraffe" story, written for her funeral service and shared here with his permission, shortly before he joined her a few years ago in their continued life (as he said) in heavenly peace.

BUFFALO AND GIRAFFE
by Wayne Tobiason, with help from Elizabeth

I don't much like it when people kid me because I am so tall, but, years ago you decided you were Buffalo and I was Giraffe. We hiked the pink rocks together, dug clams and watched the sun set over Seal Cove. Little buffalo fit just right in the lap of big Giraffe.

You proved that a buffalo could be a good skier and a great swimmer. We gave each other presents at Christmas and you saw Giraffe cry after his mother died. Giraffe seldom cries. Giraffe is crying now.

Giraffe's three daughters gave him his second youth. Your mother and father helped raise them. You became their little sister.

You and your brother and cousins gave Giraffe his third youth. We had some wicked good wrestling matches. But two sets of parents worry about an old Giraffe and a little girl's interests change from wrestling to reading. You absorbed Anne of Green Gables, visited Avonlea and talked about her adventures not in sentences but in one long continuous breath.

Giraffe and his wife got great pleasure out of watching Buffalo develop into an organized, disciplined, self-motivated individual. They began to understand why you chose to be Buffalo. They felt that a small part of you belonged to them.

You carried flowers at the wedding of their daughter, as her sisters had when your mother and father were married. Buffalo and Giraffe danced that night away.

Giraffe and his family looked forward to seeing some other little girl carry wildflowers at your wedding. But now that will not be possible. On the way to teach other little Buffalos to swim you went instead to heaven. Now the eyes of Giraffe will always see you as a little girl. Having a beautiful youth caught in your eye is not a bad thing for an old Giraffe.

Sweet dreams little Buffalo.

Sleep in heavenly peace Heidi Louise.

Buffalo and Giraffe, 1983

Life Changed

My Experience on June 10, 1994

Writings from 1998

O n June 10, 1994, getting up seemed as if something one did with-out having to think about it. That would be the last day that I took that for granted. I had been substitute-teaching at Heidi's middle school. I had a few weeks between my school year job of running an alternative school for high schoolers and adults and going to Camp Calumet to drive the boat all summer and be at camp with my kids. Substitute-teaching was a fun change. I was having a good time being in the classroom again. I was also in the middle of an intensive graduate school program to become a mental health counselor.

Heidi wasn't sure whether she liked it when I was at her school. I could feel her conflicted feelings of "it is fun to have my mom in my school," and her pre-adolescent "what if my mom does something to embarrass me?"

I raced home to meet Heidi and her friend Becca, to pick up Hans, and head for swimming lessons. Heidi and Becca, already good swim-mers, were to help with the little kids with swimming lessons. Hans was taking lessons, which was particularly important because we were to be at Camp Calumet all summer. Heidi, eleven, and Hans, six, would spend time at the family beach without my presence as a trained life-guard. I needed to know they were as well prepared to be swimming without me there to watch over them as they could be. Other moms and dads would take turns keeping an eye on our staff children. It is our job you know, to watch over our children . . . keep them safe . . . at all cost . . . our responsibility. . . . Or so it seemed. . . . Somehow we think we are all powerful and can and should keep them safe from all. Not until much later did I find out that the two girls were in Heidi's room having a very serious conversation about dying. . . . During that discussion, Heidi volunteered that, if she were to die, she would not be scared because she knew she would be with her Aunt Louise, who had died a few years earlier. Her friend made it clear that dying was a scary thought to her.

Before setting off, I quickly called to touch base with my friend Carolyn, who was to meet us to go to the swimming lessons and my mom for whom I was dropping off an exercise bike. As we got in the car, Heidi, uncharacteristically, jumped into the middle seat in the far back of our family van to be closer to her friend. I reminded her that the shoulder straps were on the ends and she knew we only used the middle (only a lap-belt seat) when the van was full. I was so sure I was making the safe decision again, because after all it was my job to keep my children safe. We headed across town to get Hans from his friend Nathan's.

My usually easy-going, good-natured Hans picked today to dig his heels in and insist "I do not want to go." So strongly!!! . . . So clear! . . . Tears! . . . Anger! "I want to stay and play at Nathan's today. I do not want to go to swimming lessons!"

These words still echo in my soul when I think of them. If only I could have listened. . . . Maybe not gone at all. . . .Nathan's mom had errands. . . . We had swimming lessons. . . . Empty wishes from a mother who wants the outcome of the day to be so different. . . . Thoughts of a child who had an intuition that his mother was not able to trust.

A few weeks later he would say, "I told you I didn't want to go." These words still come back to haunt me from time to time.

Off we went to swimming lessons with my angry child in the front seat next to me and chattering girls in the back. THAT swimming lesson plan was not to be!!!!!!

As I approached the place in the road where the turn goes to the bypass to my mother's home, my intent was to continue straight—not to go that way. I started to go straight . . . how different the day would have been . . . my life would have been . . . our lives would have been.

At the last second, I turned my car toward the Exit 9 bypass. It was as if something bigger than me . . . bigger than life . . . grabbed my car and pulled it back to that bypass and along a road that changed all our lives . . .

FOREVER.

Little did I know then that in a few short moments my wonderful world would explode. . . . By the time we neared Exit 9, we were all singing together the light summer songs of the Caribbean. When we pulled up to the toll booth, I reached to give my toll and continue on when. . .

LIFE CHANGED.

I cannot begin to describe the volume of the noise that still echoes deep inside me. I yelled "Oh Shit!," knowing we had been hit and thinking of the inconvenience of a small accident . . . how it would change our plans. In that momentary flash, I was only aware of the minor inconveniences that having to change a plan can cause. It wasn't until later that I learned that my whole life was about to change in that split second . . . deafening sound . . . crash that altered our lives. Next, I opened my eyes to see my daughter half in and half out of our van . . . lying there helpless on the pavement . . . not moving. I know I screamed for help for her. . . . I then left that place. . . . Although my body could not and did not move. I went with her for a few moments . . . minutes . . . however, was and remain sure of who those two people were. I was transported from the chaos of the accident scene to a calm, peaceful life transition with Heidi. I felt warm, comforted, and assured that she was safe, so assured that, later, when I found out the reality here on earth's plane . . . I was shocked. I did not understand then what has become so clear with time. As I watched Heidi's spirit walk off with her Aunt Louise and Bill, I felt a great peacefulness. I had a vision of Hans and Becca standing off to the side and became very aware of their safety, although in a very different way. The reality is that they were of course not standing by themselves off to the side, but somehow I knew they were OK. That was the part of this image that was important for me that day.

I was pulled back to the accident scene by the need to give people phone numbers to call crucial people: David, Heidi's and Han's dad, and Becca's mom. In my darkness, I was able to provide those numbers. I remember seeing only brief parts of the afternoon.

I have a picture of seeing the man in the truck that hit us, looking down from his big truck at the scene he had just created . . . at the lives he had just changed forever. He had a cold that day. He had taken over-the-counter medication and had started driving his truck on the highway. He fell asleep. He woke up only in time to swerve his truck to one part of my van instead of the whole van. His intent was to miss us, yet, instead, the corner where Heidi was sitting is where his truck crashed. His truck collided with that seat into which I had buckled her so safely, keeping her safe, I thought.

David arrived. I heard his voice and felt his comforting presence. We went by ambulance to Maine Medical Center, and during the ride, I thought I heard them say they had a heart beat (at that time, I was sure that meant Heidi's and she was okay). . . . I knew she was okay. I just didn't know what kind of okay then.

Friends surrounded me. A doctor came. I knew what his words were before he said them. . . . "We did all we could" . . . "tried every-thing". Others talk of my scream at that moment. I do not remember it. My mother later talked of coming, bracing herself that we were hurt, but remembering our friends who, a year before, had pulled through a bad car accident, telling herself that we would be OK, only to hear my scream announcing a very different story. A friend asked, should she take Hans home? He was OK. Just one wound that needed stitches, as if this were just a visit to the hospital and we would pick him up on our way home to the safety of our little family. Then, this beginning nightmare would be over. One wound, yes, but not the one that was healed by stitches, but the one that will keep reopening his whole life.

I couldn't go home. David sat nearby and we just went through the motions . . . I'm not sure what they were. At some point, I asked him and my dad to go and get Hans and be with him, because, that night or the next morning, I had to have surgery to have my left arm put back together. I couldn't go home to comfort my little boy.

My friends kept coming. They stayed close. Their closeness, love and care, circled around me. I was being held by so many. The hospital staff rolled me out the door so I could have surgery across town. All my friends came. I am aware of a big crowd staying with me, not leaving me alone. I remember orchestrating who would come with me and who would drive cars . . . still imagining that I had some control of my world. Friends filled my room at Mercy hospital. When it was decided that Carolyn would stay with me for the night, we asked a nurse if that was OK. She apologized for not being able to get enough beds in the room for all my friends. We said we needed only one bed and looking relieved, she said, "Of course".

Later, I received a supportive note from a woman down the hall, who had heard my crying. I don't remember . . . so many parts that I did not remember . . . parts that I am still filling in now, years later. I went into a sleep that I am sure was drug-induced . . . not yet fully taking in the reality of my day, my loss, and my forever changed life.

~~~~~~~~~~~~

Reflections from 2018

In my description above, I wrote that I knew deeply that Heidi was OK and I was stunned to hear from the doctor that she had died. These two truths did not fit for me. My agonizing scream was heard all through the emergency room when I was told.

So focused was my attention on her at the scene that my son would a few weeks later ask, "Mom, how come you were yelling for them to help Heidi and not me?" (I have no conscious memory of yelling for them to help her.)

"I knew you were going to be OK, but I knew Heidi was hurt more and needed their attention quicker," I answered hastily and with certainty. Thank God he asked, is what I have told myself many times, over the years, and thank God I knew the answer. His young literal interpretation must have been that I didn't care about him. Though I knew the answer, I also know that message sat in his body. Of course, I did and do care for and love him. The depth of that care and love is bottomless. I made no conscious decision in that moment, yet, intuitively, I had to focus on her in order to see her through her transition. We love our children, all our children so deeply. We all make mistakes and have regrets and yet hope that the deep love we have is the lifelong message they hold in their hearts from us. I am thankful every day for both my children and my love for them.

WAIT. . . . Perhaps this does not make sense to you. First, I said I knew Heidi was OK; then I answered Hans that I knew she was hurt more. Now, I want to add "in that moment." His pain is something he will carry through his life journey. I knew he was hurt physically and I know he has deeper emotional hurts. Survivor guilt is deep and real. It changes throughout life. Even in that moment I knew that he too would be OK. Thankfully, in a different way than she. Both truths for both my children were and are true.

On the way to the hospital, I felt a calmness that I cannot logically explain. Somehow I felt a knowing that both my children in their own ways would be OK. That does not mean I was not recognizing the pain that each of them experienced in their own way. My life has meant maintaining a balance of those two truths. My daughter died way before I wanted her to. I don't like that. I didn't and don't want that to be my story, her story, her dad's story, the story our son has had to live with. Yet, it is.

My children are both OK. In very different ways. My daughter lives on and shows me that often, in her new ways. My son has grown to be a wonderful, loving human being, who has had to keep working on his trauma at each developmental stage in his life.

I am thankful that the spiritual experience of that day, my foundation in my faith and my spiritual communities, my many years of therapy, my supportive friends and family members have all helped me to be in my life since that day. I will expand on the spiritual part of that day and beyond later in the section entitled "Spirituality."

Cindy Mitchell Perkins

Ups and Downs: What Helped

(Written in 1995)

Not having to work was helpful to me,
yet, being able to contribute when I could
Was healing too.

Letting myself cry. . . .
As if I had a choice.
Hugs. . . .

Letting myself smile
and laugh . . .
without being judged.
Hanging onto the spiritual experience
I had at the accident scene.
Allowing myself to believe it was as
real as it felt.

Other people talking about her . . .
sharing their memories.

Going to grad school classes . . .
allowed me to believe I
could go on.

Watching my son . . .
his innocence and play. . . .

My first laughter. . . .
Realizing I could and had to smile again.

Music was soothing. . . .
I searched for songs with
comforting words.

Allowing myself to be cared for . . .
as I was always the caregiver.
Something that I felt I had no choice but to do.

My faith . . .
both in its strength . . .
and the freedom to question.

Seeing her friends . . .
was double edged. . . .
Hard, and yet somehow I knew even then . . .
they were a way I would keep her alive.

Community:
Both at camp and at home

Place in the sun
8-17-94

How do I continue in my life now?

If you have gone through a similar tragedy, you will ask yourself, "How do I go on and how do I take in this horrific reality?" Many days, you may lay in bed wondering, "How do I get up? Or even not ask, but rather say to yourself, "I'm not getting up. I can't believe this is me and my life. I don't know how to do this." You will know your life will never be the same.

Below are some of the forms "going on" took for me. I tried many things, some familiar, some new.

When we have children they come with all the hopes and dreams that we imagine. They come with the fears of responsibility that we call parenting. We believe that they are our responsibility to care for, comfort, nurture, and most of all keep safe. We believe we can do that and we are terrified that we won't. When their life is shortened for what-ever reason, we naturally feel responsible. Somehow we have failed when anything happens to them. We believe that at our deepest core. There must have been something we could have done. If there had been, we would have done that. We so want to rewrite this part of their story and ours and have the ending not be this.

I am here to tell you that you can and will go on. I am not saying it will be easy. It is not. It is one step and moment at a time in the begin-ning and sometimes you go back to those baby steps again.

I want to say that I am deeply saddened to know that you are reading this because it most likely means you too have lost your precious child. I wish no one else had to ever make this journey through the rest of their lives without their child. I often like to say that my magic wand isn't working, but, if it were working, I would wave it over you to take away the pain and grief. I can't tell you how to handle your loss. I can share how I have grieved and how I continue to walk through my life. My hope is that, in reading about the various approaches that I tried, you might find something that is helpful to you.

I am walking, breathing, laughing, and living my life while still holding in my heart the loss of my eleven-year-old girl some twenty-nine years and more later. In the beginning, there were those who helped me. They were other moms who had lost their children. First, there was the neighbor who had lost her sweet girl just a year before my Heidi died. They played softball together as young girls. Caoimhe also died suddenly, without warning. Her parents, Anne and Ciaran, took that walk down the street, only days after Heidi died, to offer comfort. What I remember continues to be most important. Anne and Ciaran walked down the street. They were standing! They were continuing on and by being able to do that gave us hope. It was not the words they said that helped. It was the act of being and walking toward us that gave me a glimmer of hope. I saw them as being a year ahead of me on this journey. They were still parenting their other children. Their children were laughing and playing with the other kids in the neighborhood and in school and on the playgrounds of our town. My son would be able to do that too. I knew it because they walked down our street and into our home with open hearts.

In my fog and the shock of those early days, I saw a path. I didn't know what that path held but I knew there was a path. My path might not be the same as theirs but there would be a path. There had to be a path. There is hope in seeing other parents still in their lives.

Over these many years there have been so many other parents, whom I have come to know. Their laughter, living life, sadness, and grief all gave me hope that I could survive this tragedy too. As time has gone on, I have reached out to other parents. One day, a few years later, as I got out of my car to hug another mom and dad who had just lost their baby boy, Caoimhe's mom pulled in, right behind me. The truth is that we all hold each other up on any given day by being there for each other.

You too can handle your immeasurable loss. I don't know what your path will be. I know you can do this, as many of us, mothers and fathers, have had to do for generations. You will feel all your feelings again, not just the heaviness of your grief. Let yourself feel all your hard feelings (as if you have a choice) and then, as you are ready, let in your other feelings too. Joy, laughter, happiness, and a purpose to your life will all come together again. They will probably feel differently than before but you will be surprised when you hear yourself laugh or feel yourself smile again. It's OK to do all the above. You haven't forgotten your sadness. We humans can carry all our conflicting emotions at the same time. It's confusing sometimes, yet we do it and we are the better for it. To cope with this baffling jumble of emotions, I used different strategies over the months and years after the accident: letter writing, journaling, drawing, creating poems.

The choice of coping mechanisms and strategies really is about balance. Finding the right balance for being in your grief and pain is critical for healing mental health. There is no magic balance proportion. Everyone does that differently. Some of us spend a lot of time in our grief, at first. Some of us need to go to work and hang onto that part of our life. Some of us can't. The truth is that all strategies are OK. The trick is finding out what works for you. You might try work and decide that you need to take more time off. You might find that you need the routine that you are used to and are able to compartmentalize your grief into therapy sessions, workout sessions, journaling, friends, or whatever time and place help you. There is no map for this. Pay attention to your heart, your beliefs, your energy, and your needs. You will find what is right for you.

LETTERS

From time to time, writing letters has helped me. Included in this section is a sample of letters written before Heidi died and then some journaling (consisting of some letters and some stream of consciousness thoughts). I wrote to her when I wanted most to talk with her. I HAD to find a way to talk to her! Little did I know that, later, she would find ways to talk to me! In those moments when I was writing I felt connected to her and felt as if she was listening. My new way of connecting with Heidi gave me some peace, as I learned to live my life without her. I include here the letters I wrote during the first days and months after the accident.

In these first few months, I wrote as if she was off somewhere and, upon her return, we would talk about our respective adventures. As time has gone by, my letters have become a way for me to say what I wish I could say to her. I still use letter writing when I lose someone I love. I still write to Heidi. I started a journal a few years later, dedicated to my mom, when she died, so I could continue to talk to her in the same way. I often recommend a journal for letter writing to my clients and to my friends when they are grieving a loved one. If this resonates for you, get a journal. Make sure to pick out a journal that honors the relationship you have with your loved one.

If you are trying to support a friend whose child has died, maybe you could get them a special journal for writing to their precious one, when they are ready. This intimate way of staying connected with a lost loved one has to resonate for each person. On a day when they feel like they can't take another step, they might pick up the journal you had given them.

As you read on, you will see how I gravitated to what seemed most comfortable and helpful on any given day.

~~~~~~~~~~~~

March 1993

When Heidi turned ten, I gave her a journal with a unicorn on the cover, intending for us to write back and forth to each other. Following is the entry I wrote in the journal I had gifted her on her tenth birthday. In my search for connection to Heidi in the few months after she died, I began, as I could, going through her things. One day, I picked up this journal with the unicorn on it and began to cry (a common occurrence in those days). The pages are now tear stained. I cried as I looked at what she had started to write.

You are as Special as a Unicorn

To My Most Special Heidi,
You just turned 10 years old! This is the beginning of a very special time. You are turning into a young woman, I am so proud of all the things that you are doing now. It is so fun to have you reading so much. I love listening to you practice your instruments. What a great year you are having in school. 4th grade has been a real growing year for you. Lots of new things to get used to. You just get busier and busier. Are you getting excited about going to Middle School next year? I can't believe you'll be going to 5th grade. Whew! You know that you'll do great there because you are so terrific! Before you know it you'll be talking about boys all the time. Which ones are the nice ones? I love you very much. Never forget how special you are and that you can do anything you want as long as you believe in yourself and do your best.
Love,
Mom

Heidi's only letter back in that journal:

Dear Mom

Dear Mom!!!!

That was all it said. Some words were erased. I longed to know what her thoughts were and where the entry might have gone, had she finished. I was hard on myself because of the good intention that never came to fruition and now there was no more time, or so I thought.

~~~~~~~~~~~~~

May 1994

I left the following letter in her school desk on parent night, a few days before she died.

Dear Heidi,

I am very proud of the work that you have done this year. Fifth grade seems to have been a great year for you. I think you have grown up a lot and learned to trust yourself more.

I especially like the way that you take responsibility for your learning. We never have to tell you to do your homework. You always seem to be on top of it.

Keep up the good work. I'm glad your goals for the summer include reading some books, doing math and writing a story. I hope fun is part of the plan!

Love,
Mom

Little did I know then that the summer of 1994 would not become reality for Heidi. This letter would be the last letter that I would write and give to her.

Not what I planned… Not her plan… Not…

~~~~~~~~~~~~~

1994, Sometime after June 10

I picked up the Unicorn journal from her tenth birthday and began writing letters to her.

Dear Heidi,
Though you never can pick up our journal again, I will write believing that you are looking over my shoulder…Listening, Buzzing

around with millions of things to do. I miss your buzzing busy-ness, your animated speech, you talking so fast that I couldn't understand you. I even miss tripping over your trumpet in the living room! I miss you messing up your room...interrupting me when I start to talk...your smile... Your hugs...Your enthusiasm for life! Mine seems to be far away right now. I will try to find it because I know you would want me to. I have to! . . . for that little brother of yours who loves you so much.

On the first page of this journal I told you how much I love you - that was a year ago. You had changed so much since then. Grown up so much. You were starting to be my friend. I was so looking forward to that and enjoying it. I was so proud of you and how seriously you were taking learning, at school, at church, at home and even on vacation. You grew so much these last few months. The seriousness with which you undertook your first communion studies. Calling me at work in your excited voice telling me how different each reading of the last supper was. I had to be 40 to even think about that. You were only 11. Telling your friend you weren't afraid to die. You would be with Aunt Louise. Thank you for that. It helps to know you believed that.

You at school this year. How hard you worked. How excited you were when you got straight A's second quarter. You Did it Again !! Straight A's Heidi. Not even A-'s this time. All A's and A+'s - You were an A+ Kid!! Your Sam Adams Report and Presentation! Your Beautiful Friend Forever story that you finished for us. A beautiful Gift.

****

(Heidi had insisted on staying up way past bedtime the night before she died because she had to finish her Friend Forever Story.)

****

I hurt so much for you Heidi and all the things I miss about you. I feel so empty inside and yet...Somehow...Sometimes I also feel comforted and a sense of peace. As though you are telling me that you are okay. I know you are. I felt that. Who were those two people? [I saw walking away with you that day] Are they really who I want them to be? I believe they were. How else could I have known that Hans and Becca were okay and you weren't and yet somehow were?...Floating... That's how it seemed to be, as if you were floating somehow supported. I was scared and helpless. I couldn't get to you and hold you. That's what Moms are supposed to do. I wanted to —-you know that.

Maybe where you are is magical like the pages of this unicorn book or even better. You truly were a unicorn. One of a kind and very special.

I miss you.

Love,

Mom

~~~~~~~~~~~~~

Written a short time later

My Unicorn Heidi,

I still cannot believe it. I don't want to believe it. It's beyond all of my believing that someone as beautiful as you could be ripped away from us. We waited so long for you. We wanted you so bad. We prayed, we waited and finally many years later we were blessed. Blessed with our beautiful Heidi Louise. You were the joy of our lives and many others. You brought smiles to so many people's faces. Your laugh and smile.

You kept me organized Heidi. How will I know where I'm supposed to be when. You were always reminding me of where I had to be and what I had to do. How will I know if I look dorky or not? I'm wearing my dorky hat. I guess I'll always be dorky...

~~~~~~~~~~~~~

July 1994

Well Heidi,

It's been almost a month and it seems like only yesterday that you were there hugging me. Going off to help kids swim. You loved little kids so much. You and Becca had just discovered your kindred souls. A Summer at Camp, Sixth grade, the parade, playing "when the Saints" on your trumpet, all the things you were looking forward to. Music camp and the Spring Concerts. Today has been really hard. I woke up and wanted to hear you in the camper. You weren't there. I went to breakfast and kept listening for you. You never came. I've wandered around Camp and you aren't here. I want you to be here so bad, maybe that is why I keep looking. I thought I took comfort in knowing how okay you are. It doesn't feel so great today.

I'm sitting here staring at my arm. It isn't working well. People ask - I really don't care. I just want you. They ask the easy part - How's the arm. They're scared to ask the part about what hurts the most and I can't tell them because it hurts more than I can explain.

I feel closer to you outside. I like walking in the stars. Are you really the breeze or the stars? I like to think so. Then you would be around me still.

People say I'm doing well. I'm not. I feel like I'm sinking in quicksand and it's closing in fast. I'm doing all the things I think I should do when they feel right. Regular stuff, crying, writing, sometimes I think it's just because I think if I do all these things maybe I'll be better. The book I read this morning said it feels like having a stomach ache all the time. It's way worse than that!!

I hurt for Hans so much. He counted on you for so much. You always had so much fun together. You took such good care of him. A game, a hug, a project, some baseball, an after school treat - those smoothies you were making with the new blender. How excited you were!

What a fun trip to Washington we had. You were so grown up. So interested in learning. How excited you were about the Asian Art Museum, the American History Museum. We found the dollhouse in the American History Museum. Remember how carefully you looked over all the rooms? How fun.

Swimming in the pool with Hans. How we will all miss that. We all had so much fun.

I miss you wearing my clothes. It was fun having someone steal my clothes and earrings.

I just don't understand. I don't understand how we could wait so long - How you could be so terrific and How you could be gone. I just don't get it. **WHY?**

I know there are no answers. Oh Well. They wouldn't help anyway.

~~~~~~~~~~~~

July 1994

Today I was thinking about all the things that you did before you died. Was God preparing you? Did you at some level know? How come you told your friend that you weren't scared to die? You said, you would be with your aunt Louise. Why the panic rush to get the story of Friends Forever done by Friday the day you died?, not the next Wednesday, the date it was due.

In counseling last week I started to think that maybe I was saying goodbye to you when you died. I can't figure out why I didn't see the car, Hans, me, or the tollbooth. I saw a flash of you, then I saw two people standing off to the side I now realize that those people would've been in the toll booth if they had been in this place. I know now they weren't, they were of another plane. I now think I was there too. However briefly, I believe I was making a major transition. I also can only describe my lack of fear for Hans and Becca by a feeling, I just knew. I knew because of those two people. They passed along a sense of peace to me.

I have made many comparisons to giving birth. I feel like you were born to a new life on June 10th. It's not the life I had planned but it is a new part of your life. I know that someday I will understand. Cousin Stu said the Beatles song "Let it be, there will be an answer." helped him. It helps me too. I know there will be an answer. I just don't get to find it out right now. Later. Now I have to take care of here. I have to take care of your Dad and Brother and Myself. You are cared for now.

I got a new book today. I got it for Hans. It helped me too. I hope it helps him. It's called Lifetimes. It talks about lifetimes all being different. Some long, Some short. Yours was shorter than we all wanted it to be. But, you did live it!! You lived every minute of it. With smiles and Joy and Peace. That was your lifetime. Can I accept that?

I hope so. I have to. I have been given no other choice.

~~~~~~~~~~~~~

July 16, 1994

You should have come out of Camp today. After your first two weeks in a row! How I wanted to hear about your overnight trip and all the things you would have done. The Plays, Arts and Crafts etc., Hillary is coming today. She will be sad that you're not here. I have new earrings that I want to share with you. Mostly I want to hear your excited voice, see your smile and have a big hug. We're going on Heidi but not because we want to. We miss you so deeply. I know you are okay and that is the only thing that gives me comfort, some of the time. You would have loved our drive up Mt. Washington yesterday. I went with Don and Peg. I could hear you worrying about the car the whole time. We flew a kite at the top. I think of being closer to you up there. I feel your presence and loss in all that I do.

Love, Mom

~~~~~~~~~~~~~

July 23, 1994

Her brother, Hans's, seventh birthday, and his first of many without his big sister planning and organizing the kids and the fun.

Today was Hans birthday, How I missed you at his party. All the little guys were there. I didn't plan lots of activities. I thought oh they will just play. I forgot that was one of the many parts that you did. You always did the organizing. You would have had a treasure hunt or something. It would have been a better party with you there. How I depended on you. I gave Hans his hockey equipment , Remember we got it at a yard sale. I will tell him, it came partly from you. You would have wrapped it better. You would have said, "Oh, Mom." Anders and Erik were there. Oh do they miss you. All the guys are helping with Hans. Alex and Hans are becoming good friends. They are good for each other. You would like that, I love and Miss You Deeply.

MOM

~~~~~~~~~~~~

September 29, 1994

Hi Heidi,

I found out last night that my friend from Grad School has died. Have you met her? Did she tell you how much we miss you. It is so very quiet at our house. Your energy was so important to our family. Hans and I talked about Easter and Leprechaun day today. I found your forgiveness note to him about the fight you had about the Leprechaun candy. I think sometimes I was pretty hard on you. I expected a lot from you. All that 1st kid responsible stuff and boy were you responsible. I couldn't have asked for a better daughter. You were so loving, joyous, forgiving and accepting. I cry hard for the growing frustrations (**tear stained page**). *All that big girl, young woman stuff you were entering. I am trying really hard to understand more, to accept that this is what is okay for you. You have moved on to another place. You lived your lifetime. I know you have so much wisdom. You are probably watching, wishing I could know what you now know. I do know pieces of it. I feel your peace sometimes and those are my better times. Maybe that's why I talk of another solar system. I think of it as very peaceful where you are. I love you Heidi - I want to hold and hear you so bad* (**more tear stained words**). *I listen and watch for you but you aren't coming - not in the way I want. Please be okay! You have to be - that's all that helps -*
Love,
Mom

JOURNALS

In addition to the letters to Heidi in our unicorn book and in my journals, I just wrote stream of consciousness and feelings and experiences. I kept a writing journal because this form of journaling was familiar to me, having journaled through many parts of my life. I filled an entire journal with writing through most of that first year. In August of 1994, I was able to go back and write a summary of what I went through those first few weeks. There also were many back-and-forths on my feelings, reliving the day of the tragedy, and taking in the reality, as I worked my way through each day, that first year and every year since. These flows emphasize how this process called grieving is not in any way linear. It is better represented by a double helix that is fluid. One moment in time you are in the deepest pain and sorrow, the next, you are feeling hopeful as you go on your journey, learning to live with your deep loss and pain.

What follows are my raw journal entries in italics and, in regular type, my reflections on these entries as I have looked back on them at various times over the years.

~~~~~~~~~~~~

August 2, 1994

Week 1 - *Anguish, loud, heavy sobbing, birthing screams, chills in the night. Images of two people floating, feelings when I reconstruct the picture of Heidi lying there. Friends and Family holding me together as I cried from my soul. Hands touching me as I writhed in the pain of my heart. Fogginess. Surgery. Planning my child's funeral. Busy-ness of Friends and Family. Time recovering with 1 or 2 Loved ones at my side. . . Healing, Comforting, Agonizing Funeral Service.*

Week 2 - Coming out of the Fog, slowly, Reality still creeping in. Hugs from Leslie and John and other friends holding me up. David and I each trying to hold on in our own ways.

****

I wrote of coming out of the fog. I read that now with the perspective of looking back and think maybe I was starting to feel again, but I think it was a lot longer before any part of me really broke out of the fog. Reality crept in with fits and starts.

****

Week 3 - Having to ground myself for Burial Service, Support Still very strong from having others around, Buried Heidi's Cocoon.

Week 4 - Camp Calumet (where I had planned to be on the Adult Staff for the summer), - Real or not real-,Struggling with how to be "normal", Do regular stuff. Evening conversation with a friend, First time I was absorbed in a non-Heidi conversation for several hours. I felt good, alive.
Feelings of guilt crept in too.

End of week 4 - I went to my weekend at Grad School. Struggled with going or not. Would David be okay if I went? . . .
Would Hans be okay? . . .
Maybe I shouldn't? . . .
I made the decision - I went - Felt ok - I needed to.
They were as ok as we all were.

****

I now wonder if it is with that decision that I started rejoining the living and realized I had to go on. I still lived and had to live my life. It was very hard at first. I really didn't want to do much. Life said "come" and I reluctantly accepted. Grad school became a lifeline for me; I grasped it as if my life depended on it and in many ways it did.

~~~~~~~~~~~~~~

August 3, 1994

I miss her so deeply and yet I feel peaceful about her well being. Some moments those feelings fit together and some moments they don't. I have to hang onto that knowledge for it is the only peace I can find right now. The incredible love of my baby girl makes the hurt so deep. I can't imagine it ever subsiding. That pain and hole will always be part of my life now, but so will the joy that was my Heidi.

~~~~~~~~~~~~~~

August 4, 1994

I missed Heidi a lot today. I felt her loss everywhere. Children laughing, swimming and playing reminded me that I would not see her do all the things she had dreamt about. Hans brought his journal to me on his own to draw in today. He did two stories. I am feeling mellow as evening approaches. I also feel the pain building again. I wonder when it will break again. Reminding myself where I believe she is now is what I do to get through those times, clinging to my faith.

~~~~~~~~~~~~~~

August 7, 1994

Church this morning was helpful. The message was to keep going. The music was hard. Communion was meaningful. I always think of Heidi's presence when I am at communion.

~~~~~~~~~~~~~~

August 20, 1994

This week I have been pretty mellow. I find myself thinking of Heidi a lot. I think of the reality of her being gone. I am having trouble letting that be real. I've been doing lots of "if only's". Going back in time isn't possible. IF ONLY it were! I could leave later, go a different way, put her in a different seat or something. I can't do that so I have to find my way to reality.

~~~~~~~~~~~~

August 20, 1994

Oh Heidi, Tomorrow is the day you should be starting Music Camp. You were so excited about this year. It's the year of the tour. You wanted to do that so bad. I look at all of your friends and think of how much fun you would be having.

I MISS HUGS!!!!

I think of school starting and you not going to sixth grade. Of Hans in first grade and at home without his beloved sister. I think of our house without your laughter. It doesn't seem possible.

I can't even imagine Christmas, Thanksgiving or even Halloween and my birthday.

I do know you are with us but not the way I want you to be.

I want to see you around every corner. I keep expecting you to come. You were such a beautiful Happy Child. I think of the joy you brought to so many people's lives. Even when you were tiny, you were the Love of My life. I have to go on but I want you to know it's not because I want to do it without you. Everything is so hard. It doesn't seem right to smile or laugh when you aren't here. I also know I have to - maybe partly to fill the hole for Hans and Dad. I'm the only girl in the house now. You left me alone with these men! I think I can handle it? I'm trying.

Love you,
Mom

~~~~~~~~~~~~

August 23, 1994

Lots of emotions - Music Camp week - Many of Heidi's friends are here for this week of resident camp at Camp Calumet. So happy to see them . . . so hard to see them . . . so wonderful to be around their energy. Every time I hear kids from the kids camp cheering and singing, I can just see and feel Heidi's bounce this week.

Saturday nite, her friends Jen, Hillary, Laura, Julie and Christine came to the campfire at our campsite. It felt good to have their young voices and empty to look at their French braided matching hairstyles and think of the fun they had doing that together. I felt that giant stomachache - wave of grief. It's those conflicted feelings again - but, mostly emptiness and awareness of dreams that will never have the chance to grow.

~~~~~~~~~~~~~

September 1, 1994

Winding down of camp. Janet (dear friend from years of camp and also in my class at grad school) left on Sunday. Sue (friend with whom I had read so many spiritual books the summer before as adult staff at camp) left yesterday. I miss the activity level of usual camp. Janet's hugs and our foolishness.

Sue's presence. She is one of those special spiritual connections. Her spiritual groundedness has grounded me more than once. We talked before she left of our ways of taking care of ourselves. Talked of it not being selfish but necessary. A must in order to take care of others. There's more for others if you are taking care of yourself. I'm trying. Nighthawk (a beautiful native american woman and friend at Calumet) came by just before Susan left and told us a legend that had that same message. How Powerful and Confirming.

Sundays Sermon: Herb Brokering told a story about a potato today in his sermon. Is the potato alive or dead when you cut it?, he asked.

The man in the story took a piece of the potato with a young boy and planted it. The man left town for a few weeks and returned. The excited boy took the man to see the potato - growing and green. If you think it's dead, it ain't.

How simple and yet powerful and true. How like my Heidi, dead, she ain't! - Just incommunicado. (Or so I thought then)

Feeling that mellow, quiet hurt today. Need to work it through. Feel better now that I have cried some. It releases a valve after the pressure builds up.

~~~~~~~~~~~~~

September 2, 1994

Labor Day weekend wedding of Giraffe's daughter Becky

I think centering prayer might help me get through the weekend. Tonight (night before weekend) was hard. I missed Heidi's excitement. She would have been jumping around and taking care of the little flower girl and making sure Hans was clear about his responsibilities as the ring boy. Everything seemed so quiet without her presence. No one said anything about her. Maybe they - like me - feel like they will break if they talk about her. I've got to try harder to be present tomorrow. I need to go to bed.

~~~~~~~~~~~~~

September 3, 1994

Boy I guess centering prayer helped! Both to start the day and to hold myself together when I needed to in the service and later. It has been real hard not to have Heidi's bubbliness around this weekend. What I am feeling is a quietness. Heidi was always bubbling over with conversation. Hans is really quiet (by nature). I miss her noise, hugs and excitement this weekend. That voice that carries through everything isn't here. I had a nice talk with Barbara T. About how we're doing. It was good to get to talk with her.

~~~~~~~~~~~~~

September 7, 1994

First Day of Regular Schedule
Nightmare - Way worse than I thought it would be and I thought it would be incredibly bad! No Heidi coming to say Good-bye each morning. The emptiness at 2:30 when my phone didn't ring at work so she could tell me about her day.
GOD I MISS HER!
One Day of Hell after another. It feels like it will never feel better. It will always hurt. I feel lots of questions about myself and If I can really handle this. How can I keep going - Holding myself, Hans and David together?

~~~~~~~~~~~~~

September 13, 1994

Post wedding weekend

Where to begin? The Pig Pile hug at Wayne and Elizabeth's when we went to their house after the wedding. Crying all the way from the wedding to their house . . . the flood of memories that overwhelmed me as I pulled in their driveway and then walked in the door. Snow forts, Christmases, Heidi's first steps chasing their cat., Kirsten, Wendy and Becky and all the years of fun. Giraffe and Buffalo and all their games.

The long ride home to Maine. Hans crying about what he would do at home without Heidi and his camp friends. (Many of those camp friends that summer were actually Heidi's friends who took him under their wing and included him in many of their activities even though he was much younger.)

~~~~~~~~~~~~~

September 17, 1994

Jumble of feelings - Missing the constant support at Camp. Holding myself together continues to be a constant process. The screaming, crying, ripped apart, break down is right on the edge. What do I do with that? I guess I have to keep holding it together when I have to and find times to let it out. Those times are harder to find.

I realized yesterday how incredibly my stress level buttons were pushed by the traffic, trucks and noise of the highway. It took a long time to calm myself down. I guess that's like that Post Traumatic Stress Stuff.

****

I, like many others, found it hard to acknowledge that I had PTSD. Somehow I was supposed to be above that. Somehow in my mind a car accident didn't qualify me for that label. After all, I was training to be a therapist. I was a strong woman.

~~~~~~~~~~~~

Sometime in September 1994

The Turtle Saga -

(represents the journey of 7 year old Hans and his pain)

Hans decided he wanted a turtle. We went to look at them. They didn't have any so we priced the equipment and he got pretty excited. We ordered a turtle. We went to get the turtle, his face fell when he saw it. It just wasn't what he expected. (I had no idea what in fact he had been expecting but it was clear it was not that turtle.)

On the way home, I realized he had been quietly crying in the back seat. I hugged him when we stopped in the driveway. He said what he really wants is a little brother. I said I thought what we all really want is Heidi. He said yes and cried more. We ended up getting a Bunny Rabbit later that night.

He loves the bunny and is excited about "Fuzzball"

****

My little guy was looking for a way to stop his pain. Somehow he had thought a turtle might do the trick. Like all of us he was reaching out to try anything that sounded like it might help. When presented with the turtle he was very clear that was not the solution. Somehow the little bunny rabbit helped in some small way.

~~~~~~~~~~~~

September 21, 1994

Where to start with my feelings. There are so many. This weekend I found some I didn't even know I had. Group Therapy class (which was group therapy experience) with half of our 15 member class) was incredibly powerful.

"Get in touch with your feelings", sounds innocent enough - but I didn't have any that I wanted to be in touch with. Someone else talked about how happy and free they felt. I was remembering how good I had

felt only a year ago. I was in such a good place last fall. So full of life. I said so many times how lucky I was. My health, my two beautiful healthy children, David, my friends, my incredible spiritual growth. I felt so alive! Now, I don't know what to feel a lot of the time.

I knew I couldn't find good feelings easily. I found deep sadness real quick. My eyes just started to pour. I couldn't stop them. I immediately felt that deep, deep sadness that feels like I can't fall into because I might not come out. Our teacher, an experienced group therapist reminded me that that is not possible, so it was okay to go to those feelings. I felt very safe and supported so let myself feel and contain those feelings. It's hard to learn to hold such incredible emptiness. I am learning though. Learning to keep myself grounded and feel those feelings is almost exciting - at least a relief. I knew I wasn't in touch with something and now feel that I am closer at least.

The rest of the group's eyes were so full of love that I could feel all their hugs. I felt a little freer. Like maybe I don't have to carry it all - all the time.

Watching and Listening to other people with deep pain that they have carried for years makes me work harder at being honest with mine, so that it doesn't hurt me and my family more than the tragedy of Heidi's loss already has.

Anger: I found it!! First I relived the accident again as I have many times. Step by painful step, I was fully absorbed (almost hypnotic) as I described what I was seeing in my mind's eye. Our teacher/therapist kept me in verbal contact and feeling safe. After describing the accident I went to a fantasy because I felt the anger so deeply. I let my anger out at the truck and the driver. This felt like a gigantic relief.

On the drive home the next day, when a truck was near me, I felt the anxiety start and then a flashback came (as they had been), then the fantasy and then a smile. I have created a new path for those feelings.

****

This was me being able to stay in the present and not slide to the feelings from the accident, but stay in the present with my current reality and get through situations that were similar. I had some understanding then of being able to create a new "road" in my emotional brain, so that I didn't have to be overwhelmed. This has continued to help me over the years.

~~~~~~~~~~~~~

October 31, 1994

We made it - We went trick or treating and Hans had fun. Thanks to good friends and neighbors going with us.

This afternoon was one of my hardest. I started down the street to meet the bus and heard a kid's voice behind me. I turned expecting to see Heidi - She was not there of course and won't be. (Or, as I reread and copy this into this book, maybe she was and I was not paying attention the right way?!?)

I walked to Becki's (Friend, Neighbor mother of Heidi and Hans's Friends Chelsea and Amy). I was crying and crying. Becki cried with me. I'm lucky to have such good friends. She reminded me it's ok to cry and not try to be "together" all the time.

~~~~~~~~~~~~~

November 14, 1994

I'm tired.

I'm very tired of feeling like I am holding the world up. Today is a day of overwhelming feelings . . .Sadness . . .Hopelessness . . .Sadness.

****

Reading these entries all these years later still brings tears to my eyes. I remember the deep helpless pain and feel it all over again. I feel it now with the perspective that my life has gone on. I now see how hard I tried to hang on and how much work it really was to be in every moment of my life. I often talk about it being moment to moment then but now realize just how much excruciating energy I was putting into the overwhelming task of each day. The emptiness and the pain are raw in these early journal entries. I also wrote about what once had been mundane activities like leaving camp to do laundry with a few good friends. Now I can see that is noteworthy because I see what an accomplishment that was. The roller coaster of my emotions was constant in my journaling. The moments went from I feel ok today, to I laughed, to sobbing and feelings of emptiness.

The support of the many friends at camp, home and at grad school is a consistent theme throughout my journaling during this time. Friends were there in so many different ways. Some were there to listen. Some were there to offer sage wisdom and suggestions. Some were there to get me to laugh. Many sat quietly holding space with me while I cried.

Much of the summer both of my arms were out of commission due to my injuries from the accident. My left forearm and hand were broken and I was working hard on physical therapy, hoping to get use of my fingers back from the nerve damage. My right collarbone was broken, so, until this at least healed enough, I had no use of either arm. My friends became expert at helping me with all my needs. This included the Calumet friends who knew how to help get my contact lenses in so I could see clearly. My Jr. Counselor friend Karen from 1970 came before the funeral and patiently sat and shaved my legs so carefully, so I wouldn't be embarrassed in my dress for the funeral. The friends who hugged just because they saw that look in my eyes. The neighbor friend Gail, who arranged for us to be fed for months. All the people from Yarmouth, Maine - our town - fed us all that time and Gail reported not one person had done it twice when I asked in December and said I could make meals myself now. The friends who drove me to get ice cream as needed, which was often. This obviously was a great sacrifice for them, as they had to get ice cream too, you know, in order to be polite.

One day sometime in August, my doctor had removed all casts and said I could now go swimming. I was at the beach with friends on a very hot day when I announced I would like to go put my bathing suit on and go in the water. I said that I could not possibly go in, however, until my underarms were shaved as there was a virtual forest there. My dear friend Janet, who has now died, was quick to offer to meet me at the showers and help. She showed up at the shower a short time later with one of our children's super soakers (a gigantic squirt gun toy). And promptly soaked me after each stroke of the razor in order to be sure to wash the forest away! I did laugh and have never forgotten that silly moment that was so needed. Laughing again is so very important. Janet and I shared many of those moments including golf cart 4 wheeling down the camp trails. (Shhhh, don't tell the then camp director, DGuy, as we were not authorized to use the golf carts.)

My brother-in-law John went through our bills, which had been put aside, and made numerous calls to companies to say why we were late and could they kindly not charge us penalties. My dear friend and sister-in-law Leslie's calm presence brought me peace. When she was nearby, I knew I was being looked after and so were our children.

In these ways and many more, my and Heidi's friends were and continue to be there for me. Her friends, many now parents themselves honor me by welcoming a relationship with them and their children. One of those friends, Amy, all these years later, just gave her new baby girl Louise as her middle name. She told our family that she chose the name in order to keep Heidi's spirit alive. Her sister, Chelsea, who became lifelong friend to Hans, now lives nearby and I am honored to love, and be loved by her, her husband and their three beautiful little boys. I love them all and know that they help me imagine and wonder what her life might have been like. Children? Partner? Working? Various Jobs? Who knows? But, Heidi's friends give me a snow-globe view into those memories that we never got to have.

Heidi's friends and classmates came by for a visit on my patio, when they were preparing to finish high school and head off in different directions. A bittersweet moment that meant the world to me. These same friends of hers and others have included me in their children's lives.

~~~~~~~~~~~~

January 21, 1995

Finding my way in my emotions. Lots of emotions in there. They keep coming to the surface. I can't hold onto everyone else's emotions too, and yet I feel I have to.

~~~~~~~~~~~~

January 22, 1995

I'm full of thoughts and emotions about Heidi today. Crying comes quickly and briefly. I need to draw. I like drawing often. Our lives are so full of loss right now. My Father in law in November and now my Mother in law soon. This brings up so many questions for me. Why? Why Heidi and then them. So close together? Are there reasons I don't get to understand? Reasons why she went first. I don't know what to think of that. On the one hand I like that there are reasons, even if I don't understand them and on the other hand, I don't want there to be reasons. Somewhere deep inside me I am sure there are reasons and yet I struggle to hang on and find comfort in that belief.

~~~~~~~~~~~~

January 26, 1995

I had an image of Heidi (while sitting with my dying mother-in- law) being there in Heaven greeting her Farfar and Farmor
Tears come…She loved them so deeply. . .
In counseling I worked through my images.
Somehow by going into myself, I feel my emotions deeply and find peace.
I felt like I had reached my unconscious and took all day to "regain consciousness". I walked around in a fog for a long time after this session.

***

Getting to know your darkest places and then finding your light is so very very true. This also enables you to let your light shine for others. I find more energy for others after a big release like that. I will always be grateful that I found a therapist who could guide me through these experiences.

~~~~~~~~~~~~

February 26, 1995

Just talked with Hans - He is sitting here drawing a picture of him and his friend going skiing with Heidi - He said his friend reminded him of that a few days ago. He shared some of his drawing journal with his friend. He really is going to be okay - That's a big step of sharing for him.

***

Hans did not like to share his grief with anyone who knew Heidi. He was very protective of his sadness and felt that only he understood. When friends would try to say to him that they were sad too, he would get very angry. Our neighborhood friend, Chelsea (between Heidi and Hans in age), who adored Heidi and was grieving her too, kept trying to join with him around their grief. He would be so angry that her mom and I had to be there when they were together and often cut visits short. - They are now grown up, best friends and have been for a very long time. During these young days it was just too hard for him to hear that anyone was missing her, because she was his sister and only he knew that pain.

I totally related to that. Groups did not work for me at first. I did not want to hear of other parents' grief. I could only hold mine and no one else could possibly understand my loss. Later, I would come to wanting to hear and read others stories but not early on.

~~~~~~~~~~~~

February 26, 1995

I had a counseling session about how good I was feeling with myself and in my own skin just before Heidi died. Better and more comfortable and self-assured than I had in many, many years. That was all torn apart in one moment. All my beliefs, my trust, my identity, my confidence - all thrown into the air to be challenged and reworked. I think I'm starting to realize that the me I found is still there but that's very scary because what if it's there but I can't find the peace I had found before. It's hard to imagine that I could ever find that kind of peace again. I can't possibly feel as good as I did.

***

I have found that peace. I am right now sitting on my Aunt Betty's deck on Swans Island and sat here with coffee this morning thinking how sitting here is when I feel the most peaceful within my soul of anywhere. This is my peaceful place. That peace is actually deep inside me but here on this deck, on this island is a place where I so easily find myself and my calm. I am peaceful inside myself on a regular basis now. I am different. I am so different from the person I was all those years ago. I like who I am now.

~~~~~~~~~~~~~

February 26, 1995

TEARS

Tears at Hans's games, from missing Heidi's games and her friends and their moms. Tears for him not having his best cheerleader there to encourage him. Realization of the losses that are greater than Heidi. Just getting to know Hans's friends' parents and letting go of many of the parents I had seen regularly at Heidi events.

Today's game - Hans's last game for this year. They lined up like the big hockey guys and then played the star spangled banner. Tears came to my eyes - they were different tears - they were those proud mom tears, reminiscent of first day of school tears.

~~~~~~~~~~~~~

March 5, 1995

A few days before Heidi's birthday

A MOMENT OF BEING GROUNDED

In class yesterday, at one point I realized I had been totally focused and present in the moment for quite a while. I wanted to cheer. "I'm HERE. I'm HERE". A moment in time to celebrate because it seemed too often I was not totally present.

Today I was wondering how many months it had been from when Heidi died. I realized 9 months - I thought how interesting it's just like a pregnancy to now - Then oh - it was a pregnancy. Then I realized she was conceived the same week that she died.

Other connections about those weeks:

A friends sons birthday the same as Heidi's

Same friend's miscarriage years before on June 10th the day she died.

Another friend with two sons. One born on June 10th and one born on March 9th

Coincidence. I think not.

****

How do you prepare and go through your child's first birthday after they have died?

I would say to you - have a plan. There is no easy way but having a plan will help, so that when you get to the day, you have steps to walk through. This includes a plan of "I am going to sit home and cry on that day." That's ok, if that is what you need to do. It's also important to give yourself permission to change the plan in any way you need to as the day goes on.

I tried so many things that first year. I spent time with friends. I spent time with my son and husband. We gave our son a gift to cele-brate him being here with us and he always got a small gift on her birthday. We made a rocket together and sent it off to heaven with messages for her. It came back, so we saved it for another year. I planned a birthday gathering with friends and family for the weekend. We sent off balloons with messages. We had a cake. Nothing felt good, nothing brought her back, but she was present in the only way she could be now and that was important to us.

~~~~~~~~~~~~~

March 13, 1995

Counseling

I talked of the past week and then of my anger. I tried hard to isolate the anger and couldn't quite grasp it by itself. I described it as a slimy ball that I would touch as it passed by me but not be able to hold onto. My hands had totally dug into my knees and would not move - they felt like they ended at my wrists. My body was as tight as a board. At the end of the session, I said "I am FUCKING pissed". I repeated it many times and got louder. My body started to relax after I said it several times. It felt great to acknowledge that I was so angry. I had not done that much up to now.

I left feeling exhausted and exhilarated - much released and relieved.

~~~~~~~~~~~~

March 20, 1995

Wow- So many things have happened - Heidi's birthday has come and gone - I put a tremendous amount of energy into honoring her that week. It felt like the right thing to do - starting on Monday I spent some time with a friend and her young baby and shared spiritual connections, talked about my wonderings, my feelings of not believing in coincidence anymore. I was in a much calmer accepting place and now all those connections make sense even though, "it is beyond the rational mind".

We went to the middle school and decorated the tree Heidi's class had planted, with her friends, in June, in her memory. We went from there to a favorite dinner spot of hers.

On her actual birthday, I stayed home and went into her room. I read many of her writings, journals, poems and stories - This was a way to feel as though I were having a conversation with her. I cried some and felt calmed some.

I went to a friend's and we cried together a lot. I went to the cemetery by myself and took two balloons - I tied mine to the tree and let Heidi's go. I went to another friend's and cried and calmed down. We talked. Hans had a friend over. He got off the school bus and was ok but when he saw my car in the garage where he was planning to play he screamed at me and cried. I comforted him and assured him I'd be glad to move the car. He calmed down then. If only his emotions were just about the car.

The next few days were dedicated to planning a gathering with friends and teachers on Sunday. By Saturday, I was exhausted and wondered why I was doing this event. I realized it would have been an exhausting week no matter what I did. I chose to honor Heidi with my energy instead of being angry and eating too much. Somewhere around 60 kids came Sunday with all her teachers, aunts, uncles and cousins too. We talked, made things, wrote memories and let balloons with our personal messages go off. The kids sang Happy Birthday to her with such clear yet sad voices. It was comforting to feel the energy and support of so many others who still miss her so much, too.

I had lit a candle on her birthday to have a piece of her spirit around for a few days. It burned until the next Wednesday morning. I had become very attached to it. I watched it every night and cried when it went out. Huge amounts of energy.

~~~~~~~~~~~~~

April 7, 1995

Next few days I lived in fear of stuckness (PTSD) happening again. I fought it off once while driving in the car. Another time I was in class and went out in the hall and sat on the floor. People talked to me. It was like I was in a bubble. I was answering in my head but, not outloud. Someone brought me water. That helped me come back to the here and now. I was able to return to class and be present. Took a nap at our lunch break.

~~~~~~~~~~~~~

April 29, 1995

Afternoon after the Softball field in town was Dedicated to Heidi

As I approach the ballfield, I hear cheering. I see green and yellow uniforms. I walk over to my place at the fence. . .where I can see my blond batter determined to swing- where she can look to me for support.

. . . before and after. . .

I stand there . . .tears streaming down my face...hearing, seeing, feeling every game I stood here for . . .3 seasons worth . . . I just stared . . .first at home plate then at the dugout . . .as if . . .if I stare long enough she'll come walking from the dugout, look to me for support and then swing, get that hit and come home with me. I cry, then walk to my car alone . . .without my ballplayer.

(A few hours later)

I drove across town in a quick downpour . . . as I looked toward her dugout I saw the most amazing rainbow coming from the dugout!!!!

The day after the rainbow

"Did you see the rainbow, Mrs. Tobiason?
Yes, I did!
"But, did you see that it was right over Heidi's field?", said the excited innocent voice.
Yes, I did! And I smiled, that bittersweet smile that has mountains of weeping right behind it.

***

Thank you to all the children and adults who saw that rainbow and continue to remind me of it to this day.

<div align="center">~~~~~~~~~~~~~</div>

June, 1995

First Anniversary Of Her Death Approaching

During this first year of my grief journey, I have been through a Group Therapy class as part of my graduate program. It was an experiential Group Therapy. I summed my experience up by saying that to be in a group experience you have to say Hello and Goodbye. Towards the end of the first year of living without Heidi, I went to Sedona Arizona for just a few days. I knew nothing about the spiritualness of Sedona. Spiritual it was. A very unexpected experience was to happen. I stopped by the Chapel in the Rock and looked over to Cathedral Rock. I was shaking and had chills, as often happened and still does when I feel Heidi's presence or a spiritual message rings true for me. I was drawn to Cathedral Rock. I found a brochure that said there was a short easy hike to the top. I went, thinking I was going on an easy climb. I climbed the side of that rock like I have never done before or after. I did not climb with my feet on the ground. I SCALED the rock in a tight crevasse thinking in just a short while I would reach the place where my feet would be flat on the ground again. They were not. I went almost to the top but did not dare to climb over the top when I got there. As I climbed I would get scared and look down and think, "what am I doing, why am I going on." I would look across to the chapel in the rock, which shows as just a cross from Cathedral Rock, and feel and hear a strong message that I would be ok and to keep going. I did until that last piece where my hand reached over to the top, but I could not get there. My message?, I could not reach the top nor could I reach Heidi in the way I wanted. THE ROCK poem (page 105) is what I wrote upon my return. The Hello (page 109) and Goodbye poems (page 111) were written after the entire two days of feeling her around me, climbing the rock, going to Oak Creek Canyon, and feeling her presence and sobbing as the sun set over the Grand Canyon.

The experience of climbing the rock in Sedona and not being able to reach the top was exactly like my experience of not being able to reach my children the day of the accident. I could not reach either of them to help them and I could not reach the top of Cathedral Rock. This experience is exactly like the experience of my hands that came up in therapy over and over again and as represented in my drawing journals.

June 10, 1995

What do you do a year later? A year to the day that your child died? For most of the month before I thought about it? I worried about it? I made some plans. I lit a candle and let it burn to keep her spirit with us through that day and actually several days until it went out. I cried hard when it flickered out a few days later. I hugged my little boy. We talked about her and remembered the good times. We all three talked about missing her. Friends and family called and came by. I went to the ocean and threw rocks in the ocean to make great mad sounds.

Everything hurt and then it was the next day. Making a plan for anniversary days has always helped me. I do not always stick to the plan but, I have a plan to fall back on as I need it. I started that the first year with the help and advice of many others.

DRAWINGS

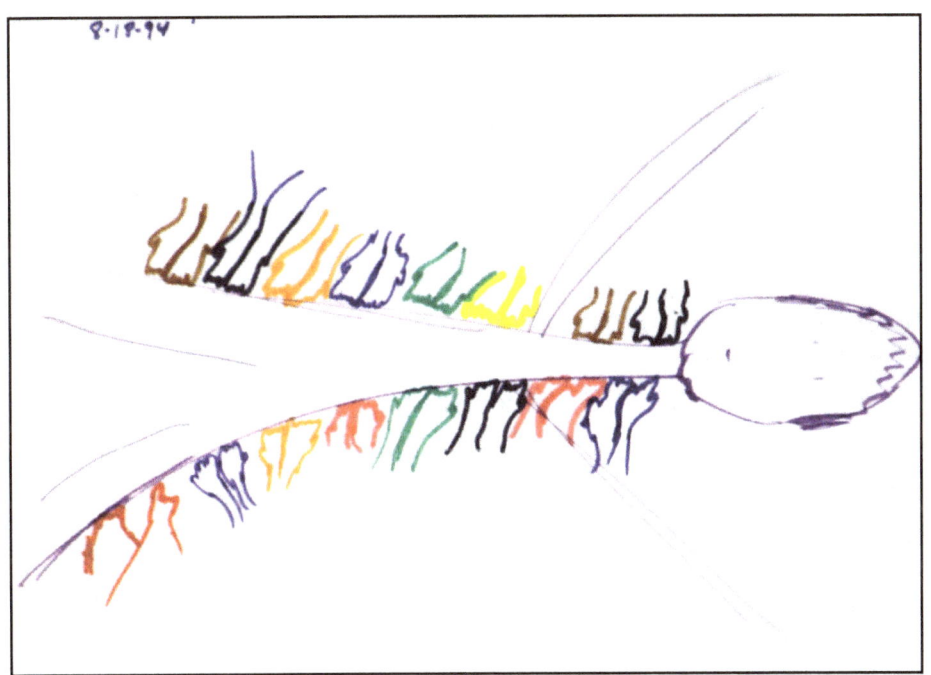

8-18-94

Hands of Prayer - 8-18-94
(Drawn two months after Heidi Died)

Another way that I processed my grief was through drawing, which was new to me. At first, I would just stare at the blank page with drawing materials in front of me. I had never done this drawing thing and certainly had lots of hesitation about a blank page. This came from old messages of "you cannot draw."

Writing in a journal was in my comfort zone, but a massage therapist I had seen suggested I try a blank page and colors. She actually would give me time and materials after a massage to do just that. I said, I can't draw—many of my clients and friends have since said the same about themselves. I tried anyway. I now give people the advice of drawing as a therapeutic method. See what happens, I tell people, just pick up a color and a medium you are drawn to.

The drawings in the pages that follow date from August 1994, just after Heidi died. The Letters and Journals sections above include entries whose dates overlap with those of these drawings. The types of journaling were kept separate, so that readers could access each type individually.

Looking at my journal entry brings back the sense I had of so many people and things that held me up. I remember feeling as if I could not hold myself up. But with the help of all the many friends and family who were there for me, I was staying afloat and afloat is how I felt. I felt far from grounded—feeling that way would take a long time. So many hands from so many parts of my life are represented by those colors and those hands: my spiritual community at Camp Calumet . . . my neighbors and friends . . . John and Leslie . . . my family . . . my son, Hans . . . David, Heidi's Dad and my husband . . . my grad school . . . my CDs . . . my walks in the woods . . . staring at the water . . . my journal (just beginning).

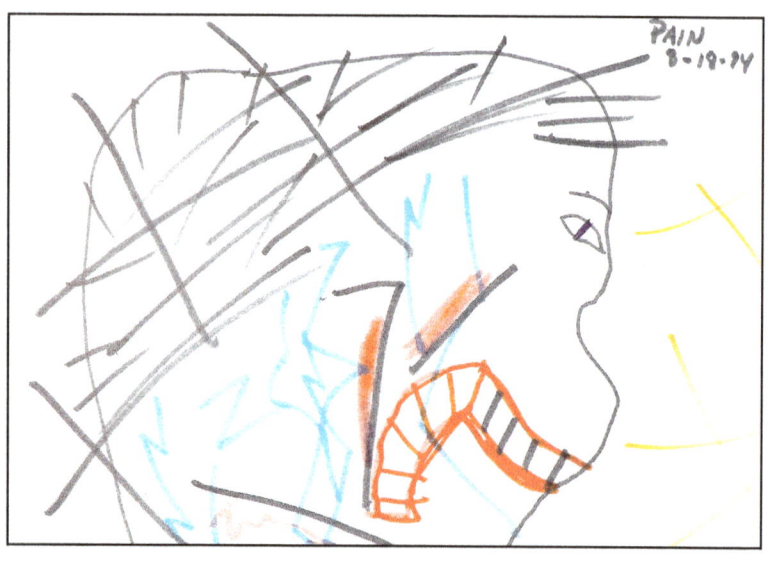

Pain; August 18, 1994

"How could you draw that?" a friend now asks. "It's hard to imagine that you could do anything," she says, wondering how I could function at all. My response to her is that, even though I felt paralyzed in some ways by the pain, I had to push through it and be willing to try anything that I thought might help, so I began. Over time drawing did help. It helped when I looked back and saw how I felt that day, two months after my greatest loss—just two months following my world forever changing.

I look at that now and remember that was me. I know that pain. I know that scar. For, now, it is a scar. Some days it hurts again. Today, I can look that pain in the eye and know that, unlike then, I know how to hold that pain. I have learned to live my life even though that wound will always be there. The pain does not sear the way it did on that day twenty-four or more years ago.

It's possible that the "Hands in Prayer" drawing, which was done on the same day as this "Pain" drawing, provided enough of a reminder of my support systems that I could then allow the pain in and this drawing to come forth to a conscious level.

Out of Nowhere; August 24, 1994
(The Millisecond that changed our lives and ended our dreams)

It was a millisecond that came out of nowhere. It changed our lives forever. I will never hear a siren, or go by an accident scene without thinking someone's life just changed forever. I pray for them and hope they are the lucky ones whose lives change in small ways. Ours changed in a giant way. A way that lives with us forever. Our blue van was hit by a delivery truck at a toll booth. Some days, I go through toll booths now and don't worry. I know somewhere in me, even on those days, there is a memory, a fear, a pain that remembers in my body, if not in my thoughts. Now, I watch behind me at tollbooths and while driving, probably more than most people do. I always want to know. I don't want to be struck from out of nowhere again—as if I can control that by being on the lookout. Up until that day, I thought I could control everything that involved keeping my children safe. I shared in the fantasy that all of us moms can control what happens, if we just do all the right things—fasten seat belts, drive carefully, watch the road, etc., etc., etc.

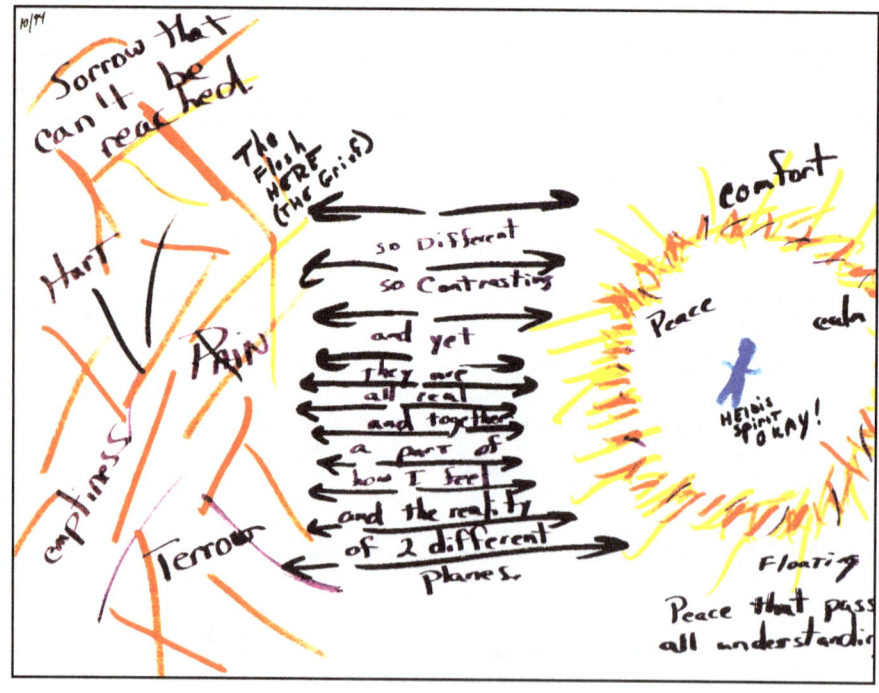

October, 1994

My day to day, even moment to moment experience. . . .
The planes of my existence that I could not bring together. . . .
Some moments I felt that peace I had felt as she was dying. . . .
I longed to hold onto that. . . .
I wanted that to make the horror . . .
and the pain not be real. . . .
I tried so hard to stay in that moment in time. . . .
YET . . .
the pain . . . hurt . . .
the sounds . . . the emptiness . . .
was real too . . .
so overwhelming at times . . .
I thought I would not ever come out of it. . . .
And yet . . .
I did. . . .
Both emotions and experiences
real . . . raw . . .
both now part of me.

I am sitting here IN MY HOUSE in peacefulness—WOW! I have changed my morning work schedule. I feel much calmer. I came home from school earlier, because I had a plan to take care of myself. I have been okay because I knew I had some time to myself. I have been able to go to Heidi's room and sit and cry for the first time. I held her precious Kirsten doll and sobbed and felt a relief from this release.

I feel like I have blown through a time warp—so many things have happened to me in the last few days and weeks. I feel like I'm back on that roller coaster of emotional shifts, like earlier in the summer, but I feel like I am driving the roller coaster now. I don't feel like my feelings are driving me as much as they were. That's pretty energizing.

***

Do these comments reflect a release of feelings caused by drafting the picture?

I am still feeling okay today. I feel like I have the energy to do whatever I have to do. I still have the image of blowing through the wall of guilt and blowing away the barriers to emotions. I feel like I am feeling again. The energy surge I felt in class lasted a very long time. I felt as if a lightning bolt was going through me, but I felt good to be in control of that for so long. I have a newfound burst of energy.

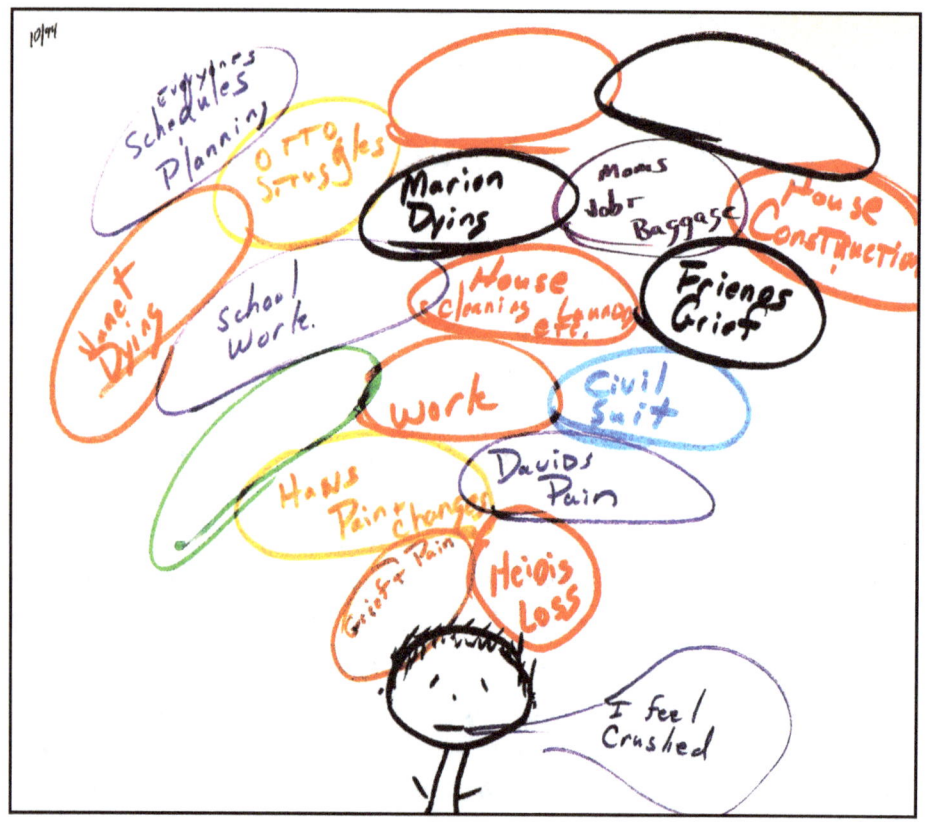

Crushed; October 19, 1994

2 days after Crushed drawing - release of feelings 2 days ago?

I also feel sadness today. My sadness has felt different somehow. I feel it there inside me but it's not pushing me to do something with it. I feel that I am holding it. I feel grounded right now.

I am sitting in the waiting room while Hans is in with his therapist. She just stepped out to say that he is really talking to her today. He is talking about how hard it is to be at our house because everyone is sad there. WOW. Big steps for Hans. He's so sensitive to feelings.

****

By October that first year (1994), I was trying to find my new normalcy, whatever that was. In my feeble attempts to return to work, get Hans off to school, enjoy him and his friends every chance I got, connect with friends, stay in grad school, etc., etc., I was met with feeling completely and totally overwhelmed. I saw no way out of it and yet had to keep getting up and putting one foot in front of the other. Anything I had to do felt like too much. I felt like everyone else wanted me to take care of them. I am now sure that I invited that in some way, possibly to avoid having to look at my own pain. The Crushed drawing shows the many things that I felt I had to carry on my shoulders. Life kept going on. I really didn't understand how that could be. In one big way, life had stopped for me. I needed to find ways to hold onto myself in the midst of everything and everyone. My writing, drawing, grad school, massage, and music were the beginning of my lifeline. They were my way of showing myself and the world that I was still alive and functioning and yet, at the same time, they were my exhaustion. I was trying anything and everything that someone suggested might help. In truth, nothing helped the way I wanted it to. Nothing was going to bring Heidi back.

HOPE. December 1994

While sitting in grad school in December of that first year (1994), having gotten through our first Thanksgiving with the help of family and friends, including having a giant neighborhood "Turkey Egg Hunt," I was doodling, and this image of a tree, butterflies, and star appeared. I had doodled what became a symbol of hope to me. A simple line of butterflies weaving their way up to the sky and this very bright star came to represent the many loved ones—especially Heidi—whom I had lost and whom I saw coming together to become this giant light in the sky. I felt hopeful in the middle of a holiday season I wasn't sure how to get through. This image I created helped me to find hope during a holiday season that felt so empty.

I also drew the second tree with balloons being released from it, representing our way of communicating with Heidi, by sending messages via balloon, up to where she now lives. More HOPE and paths to navigate this season.

Christmas 1994

Every Christmas since 1994 has been mixed. This picture, drawn that first year, tells so much about that journey. My focus that year was very much on trying to make sure seven-year-old Hans had a magical Christmas, as all children should have. I still have the clay Santa and reindeer that he made at his therapy session, and then, we created the rest of the reindeer at home together. All the years thereafter have witnessed many superglue moments with antlers being attached back on. The tree is now filled with many wonderful ornaments that represent memories of his growing up and the precious ones that were gifts for

76

Heidi and others that her little hands created. The angel at the top is the angel that she and I created for the Christmas of 1993, not knowing that would be her last one celebrated with us. Somehow we got through that Christmas. I now look forward to the holiday season and, sometime during the season, I pay attention and honor the loss of having Heidi to celebrate with.

That first Christmas, in 1994, friends and family once again held us up. Family friends, whose boy was a friend of Hans's, invited us all over to have Christmas dinner and time with them that day. It helped Hans to have a friend to be with that day and it was helpful for us to be with other people and not be in our house all day. We did a balance of being in our home and going with these friends, to be near the old memories and begin creating new ones. There is no magical answer to these most difficult days and times of year.

Each year, as I place her angel on the tree, I take a moment to call her in and smile as I think of us putting it on the tree together. Tears usually come and then turn into a smile, as I have both conflicting feelings every year.

Sharings and Learnings; January 25, 1995

It's interesting to me as I look at this drawing, from the perspective of many years later, that I had placed a dream catcher at the top of the drawing.

I'm sure it was meant to represent the love of Native American traditions that Heidi was exposed to at Camp Calumet during the summer of 1993 and that she adored sharing. She embraced those traditions fully and completely. She loved and respected our friend Night Hawk Flying. She became very insistent on showing respect for our Mother Earth and taking care of our environment.

The other symbols in the drawing stand for the many things that she brought into my life and her brother's life. They also represent the things that I shared with her and her brother. Our faith, Christmas traditions, water, imagination (especially the fantasy of Disney), music, art (something I learned to appreciate from her), bike riding (we had gone on a long-distance bike ride together and she had planned to join me on the Trek Across Maine a few years later), books, love of children (her brother being the most important one).

I now see the dream catcher at the top of the drawing and realize the sketches below also represent so many dreams that never got realized. They only began so briefly with her here on this earth. I continued fulfilling many of these dreams with Hans as he grew up. He talks of not remembering her, yet I see the essence of who she was in him. I also continue to pursue some of these dreams within myself.

Writing this book is one of these dreams. This is the one Heidi and I had promised to do together and we now are doing just that. We're not writing it in the way I had imagined so many years ago, nor is the topic what I had thought it would be, but she is here with me every time my fingers place themselves on the keyboard to continue crafting this book.

My Ruby in the Room of Gems; February 5, 1995

February 8, 1995

During my reiki/massage session this week, I felt energy moving again. It feels so much like in my counseling session, when I reach a deep place and also feel energy moving through my body. Is it because I am touching my unconscious or connecting with other energy sources?

Carol (my Reiki and Massage therapist) then led me on a visualization to a room filled with gems. I was immediately struck by a large red gem - Ruby - When she told me I could choose any gem in the room, I tried to talk myself into other gems. BUT the red ruby would not go away. I felt something about my mother come into the picture too. After the visualization, Carol said people often go right out and get the gem of their visualization. I did not need to, because I already have a ruby ring that my mother gave me on my 21st birthday. This ruby seemed to be giving off immense energy that I have felt again - filled inside with energy since then.

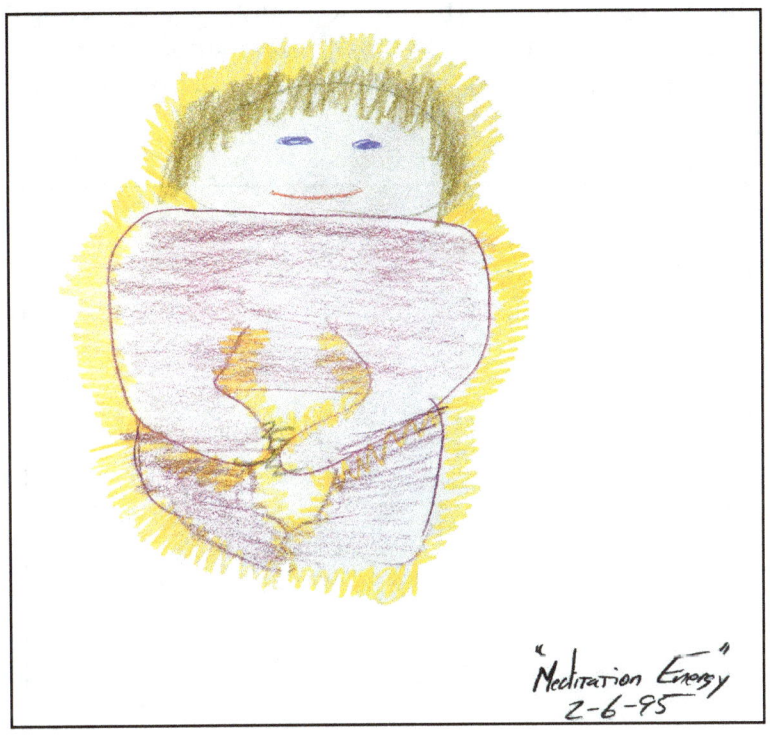

Meditation Energy; February 6, 1995

Meditation became a healing/calming place for me.

February 8, 1995

ENERGY!? ENERGY!? ENERGY!?

Energy – What does it all mean? Where does it all come from?
As I meditated last Tuesday, I felt an intense pouring in or filling up
with energy. I had felt totally empty and then found I had plenty of energy
after meditation. I felt a letting go and then a filling up. This meditation
happened about an hour before my mother in law died. Coincidence? - I
don't think so.

Cindy Mitchell Perkins

I completed this drawing a year after Heidi had her tonsils out. A month after I made this picture, I sat with Hans in the same waiting room and wrote the poem "That's What Moms Do," reflecting on this day with Heidi, as I waited for Hans to have surgery with the same doctor. "That's What Moms Do" is found in the "Poetry" section of this book.

You were so alive; Tonsil Day; 1995

I was asked to visualize my loss as an animal or a thing. I visualized this gigantic purple dragon. These are my first two drawings of the dragon. I am in both pictures as a tiny speck of a person. Over time, this visualization changed (in the middle of the day, the image of a dragon would just pop into my head—but transformed little by little). Eventually the dragon and I were eye to eye and I stared the dragon down. It no longer had control of me. I was in charge of myself and the dragon.

Me staring down the dragon has become a symbol of strength for me since then. I have a small purple dragon tattoo that symbolizes my strength and reminds me what I can handle when things get hard.

Purple Dragon; March 2, 1995

Purple Dragon: As peace came, I grew; March 3, 1995

Coming to Life; March 15, 1995

Signs in my drawings that I was feeling better and having hope again.

This drawing really shows how up and down my feelings were. Just after getting through what would have been Heidi's twelfth birthday, the first one celebrated without her, I was able a week later to feel some hope. These ups and downs continued, yet this was a day when I could access hope and be more present in my life.

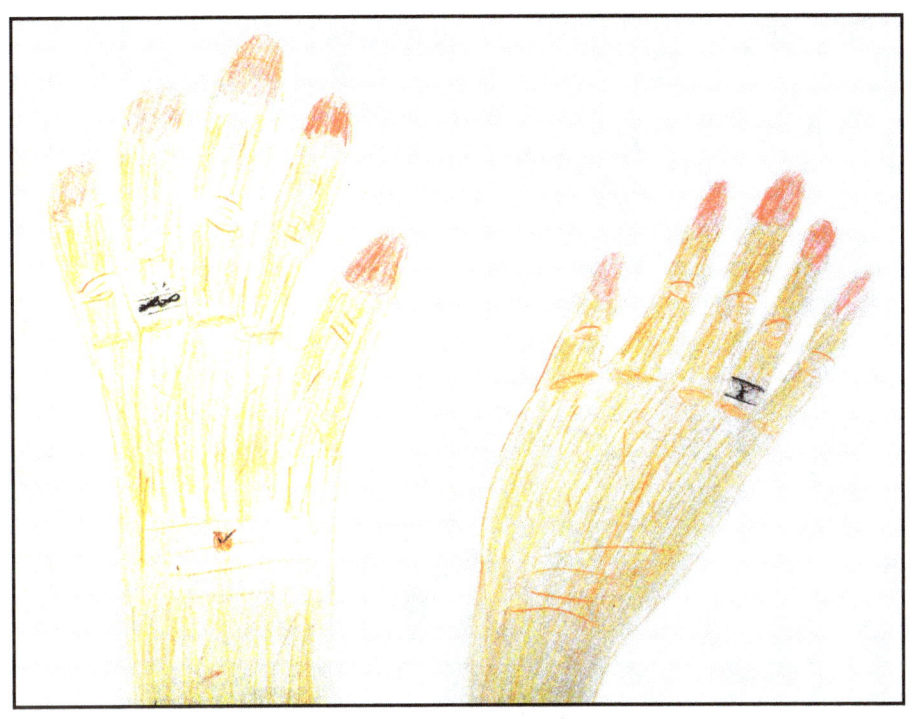

Distorted Hands—Why? March 22, 1995

March 20 1995

I visualized one hand was bigger than the other. one hand being swollen. I sat with my hands on my knees - very, very tense.

It became clear that something was going on with my hands and I had drawn hands in my drawing journal. I was not sure what this was about. I could not move my hands. My therapist helped me focus on my hands and try to move them. I could not. Finally, she asked if this is what it felt like when I tried to get to my kids at the accident. It was like a dam burst. I wept and nodded. I felt like I was in the car again - trapped. I calmed down and talked of what I remembered.

Then, this drawing came:

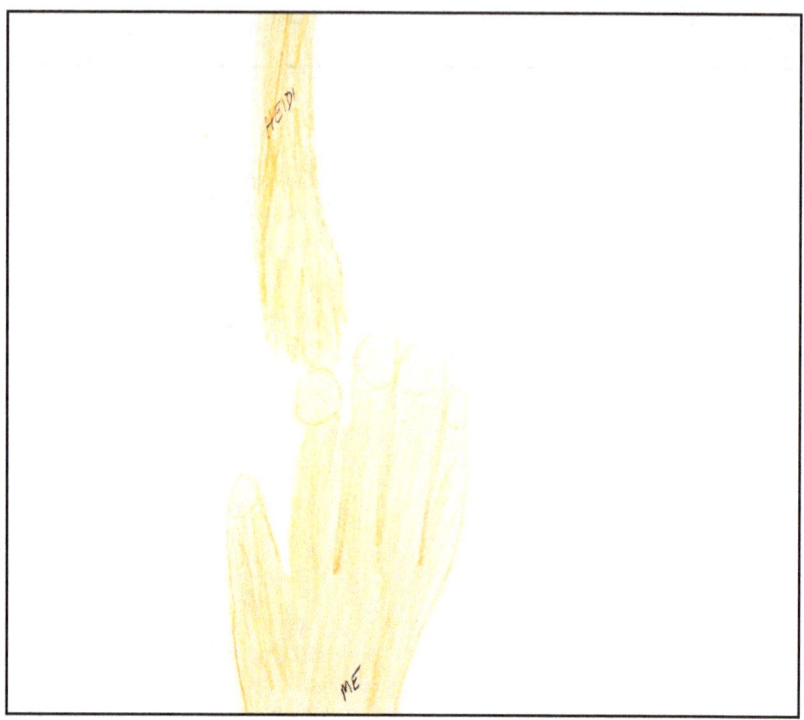

Almost but not quite; April 6, 1995

I could almost get to Heidi, but not quite. She wasn't within my reach.

Early June 1995

Hands again - I looked at my hands after I had said that Stephanie (my therapist) looked big and I felt very small. She said to show her how small. I put my hands together and said small enough that maybe I could be held in someone's hands. I then looked at Stephanie and said, but there aren't any hands big enough. I think maybe there are - God's hands. I feel that happens through the love of all my loving and caring friends - that image of being held by so many hands that I drew a while back.

Next few therapy sessions

I spent the next few sessions experiencing the emotions of June 10th and finding them in different parts of my body. The most powerful feeling was that of being stuck and not able to get to my children. I couldn't move. I would freeze in my sessions just like I had on that day. My therapist would carefully walk me out of it and help me to remember that this was a different day. She would lead me through breathing exercises to breathe the stuckness out of my body. I spent some time in fear that I would get stuck again. My therapist gave me strategies to stay in the present when I felt this coming on. One approach involved using my senses to remind me of the present. For example, people who knew me well could help by asking me questions like, What color is my shirt? Or, they could offer, "Here, have a glass of water," or anything that got me to come back to the present.

During this time, I was very aware that part of me was struggling with memories that I could not find. I did not know exactly what happened during that stuck time. I know I was physically stuck in the vehicle, but do not remember details. By getting to the experience of those body memories, I was able to let those panic feelings go.

Cindy Mitchell Perkins

Cindy gazing toward Cathedral Rock

POEMS

Sometimes, I would sit down and poems would flow out of me. This process was cathartic for me in a way and became another path for learning to live with my grief. I would often write a poem and think that it didn't sound like much, but I felt in some small way a relief or a little lighter. Later, I would read the same poem and think, WOW, I wrote that? It was as if I did not recognize my own voice and depth of feelings.

I think now that sitting in these feelings through the many forms I used was such a release that I have not held the conscious memory of the depth of the pain. I sat in it, walked through it, and then moved on. Many times, over the years, I have circled back through the pain again, but each experience I believe has been a little different. Some experiences felt less intense, others just more familiar and, with that, comes a knowing that I will move through my feelings once again. I will be able to continue on and know how important it is for me to pay attention to the pain when it is present, so that I can also be in the joys of my life when they come along. Without the fullness of my pain when it is in my face, I would not be able to fully be in the joyful moments of my life.

Cindy Mitchell Perkins

What Am I Afraid of?
(1994)

I don't know where to begin. . . .
I am afraid of my grief. . . .
It's huge.
I am afraid that I somehow will not recognize it
and it will hurt someone I love.

I am afraid of more loss.
I am afraid that somewhere out there
in the rest of my life
is another trauma.

I am afraid of my own sanity.
I'm afraid that I don't know when I am
okay and when I am not.

I am afraid of my emotions.
I am afraid of their intensity. . . .
When I cry from my gut,
I'm afraid of scaring someone who hears me.

I'm afraid of anger.
My own, when I direct it at someone I love
because I am afraid that
I will scare them away.

I am afraid of their anger at me
because I am afraid that they will
go away or never come back to me.

I am afraid of cars.
I don't want to get in one today.
I don't want anyone I love to be in one.
I'm afraid of other drivers.

I am afraid to let people I love out of sight,
as if I could protect them.
I am afraid of holding on so much that I lose them.

I am afraid of not finding my alone time again.
I used to love it.
I am afraid to slow down and especially afraid to stop.

I am afraid of doing too much as caretaker
and not taking care of myself.

I am afraid of other people's judgment.
I am afraid of losing my dad.
I am afraid of hurting him.

I am afraid of getting on my bicycle.
I am afraid of an accident.
I am afraid of not finding the love and peace
I have always found on my bicycle rides.

I am afraid of big trucks.
I am afraid to be angry at the truck driver.

I am afraid of not having enough money.
I am afraid of not being able to do a good job
this year.

I am afraid of the dark.
I am terrified of life being cut short.

I am scared of flashbacks and noises in my head,
that won't go away sometimes.
I am terrified to look at that moment in time
when there was a crash and all the laughter stopped.

I am afraid to be happy.

Cindy Mitchell Perkins

Who Will You Be?
(December 31, 1994)

A teacher . . . you said
"I want to be"
Not a President
like Lindsay
or a Lawyer
like Becca
"A Teacher Mom . . .
it's so important"
helping kids like
you do

So many people
have learned so much
from you, Heidi
Me . . . about living
Friends . . . about happiness
Moms . . . about priorities
Many . . . about faith
Family and others . . . about caring
Groups of kids . . . about creating change
All of Us . . . about loss and trusting
A teacher
you are

Hans
Pain, Sadness, Emptiness

(February 4, 1995)

I learn step by step
day by day
to hold all the
feelings . . .
all the loss.

I watch you too
trying to understand
holding your feelings too.

Mine feel too great for
my grown-up personhood
How can your seven-year-old
person hold them all?

You work so hard
thinking, feeling, asking
I am so proud of you.

I want somehow to do
it for you.
Travel the path of pain
that you wouldn't have to.

Cindy Mitchell Perkins

You should be laughing, playing ball
and thinking of fun things.
But that is not to be
all of
your path my child.

I learn step by step
day by day
that you have to travel
your own path
and I—your mom
can only watch, learn
and be there to lean on
as you are ready.

Your First Goal!
(February 4, 1995)

SCORE! First real hockey game
First goal!
WOW—What a triumph!

A moment of joy
amidst so much sadness.

You seemed to forget for
a moment and soak in
some joy.

Too soon you seem
quiet and sad again.

What's behind those quiet
eyes?

Does it somehow not seem
right to you
that Heidi's died
and you are smiling?

It is right, little guy
for you to smile
and feel the joy
of your first goal.

What isn't right is that
there should be any
hesitation in that joy!

Take a turn in your road
and touch the joy
that is you again.
You deserve it

That's What Moms Do
(February 7, 1995)

Dear Heidi,
Today Hans and I sit
waiting to be called in
his pre-op ear tube appointment.
He plays your Game Gear
a gift for this day last year

We sat there together
waiting to be called in
Your tonsils needed to come out.

You were so fun to be with that day.
Playing your new Game Gear
not worried that they seemed to take forever
to call you in.
My job to worry
That's what moms do.

We talked of school
your upcoming birthday.
So relaxed
so easy

Hans and I talk about
his hockey goal
mostly he plays your games.

I got up to see
if they had forgotten you
They had.
The nurse came looking
your doctor was ready.

You had to change quick
then were whisked into the OR

Keeping Heidi Close

I gave you a hug
told you it would be okay
That's what moms do.

I worried
wondered
You came back
minus your tonsils.

I will worry tomorrow
for your brother

I hugged you
comforted and held you
I brought you home
fed you popsicles
That's what moms do.
You were so alive
that day.

Today I looked
at those two empty chairs
where we sat just one year ago.

Today I can't hold
you or comfort you.
Today I miss you.
Today I cry.
That's what moms do.

Tomorrow your brother will sit here
be whisked away
come back with
tubes in his ears.

Same place
same doctor

Tomorrow I will hold him
comfort him
tell him he'll be ok
feed him popsicles and ice cream
That's what Moms do.

Cindy Mitchell Perkins

The following poem was written for the occasion of Heidi's first birthday since the tragedy, March 9, 1995.

THE WORST LOSS?

**My response to Barbara Rosof's The Worst Loss:
How Families Heal from the Death of a Child**

March 2, 1995

Same? . . . Different?
More? . . . Less?
Worst?
I don't think so

Too much alike
Pain is pain
Loss is loss
Grief is grief
It all hurts till you scream.

Loss of
parent . . . child . . . friend . . . sibling . . . spouse
mental functioning . . . physical functioning . . .
limbs . . . senses . . . dreams . . . hopes

They all rip apart your dome of protection
your magic
your fantasy that you can
protect and control
somehow take care of
yourself and those you love

They all take
grieving . . . anger . . . denial . . .
guilt . . . spiritual searching . . . going on
if only and . . .
sometimes acceptance

We cannot pretend to know or rate another's pain and loss. . . .
We can only feel our own.

So, differences?
Yes
But worst?
I don't think so.
I don't know how to measure.

Prelude to Wolves

Somewhere in that foggy first year after losing my Heidi
near what should have been her twelfth birthday . . .
actually it was her twelfth birthday . . . just not
the way I had planned . . .
but rather a gathering of her friends and family . . .
remembering . . .
crying . . .
hugging . . .
laughing . . .
joined together . . .
sending off twelve balloons . . .
to her heavenly birthday

I found and read an article. . . .

In "The Wolf at the Door" . . .
John Hensley
describes the moment to moment
experience of a changed life . . .
where your innocence is gone . . .
your belief in parental control . . .
is taken away. . . .

I was searching for a way to be in the world . . .
a new way to define myself . . .
I too, like John and his wife Jan . . .
was a therapist . . .
albeit in the making at that point.

I re-read the article . . .
and my response . . .
as I approach her thirty-fifth birthday . . .
I had so merged our stories . . .
my memory was we both lost children . . .
we did not. . . .

Our outcomes were not the same and yet . . .
many parts of our journeys were. . . .

We both had to learn to live with
a wolf in our lives. . . .

Cindy Mitchell Perkins

My Wolf
(March 19, 1995)

"A wolf at the door?", you say
"NO", I say.
The wolf is in my home . . .
my life . . . my very being.
Sometimes the wolf is right
where I can see it
in my face
sometimes it slides to the side
or another room and then
WHAM
as if from nowhere it leaps
and lands
so that I'm flat on my back again.
I get up reeling then
catch my breath
go on with my life
in my new cautious, precarious way.

The wolf slides back into the distant fog.
Maybe it's hiding in the attic?
I act as if everything is ok
I move faster
as if
it's gonna leave me alone
this time.
Firmly saying
but not quite believing
"so what, you're there and I
won't let you bother me
WOLF!!!

Then
it stalks
ever so carefully
lets me string out a little further
I start to find hope again for me
and others
though shadowed by my wolf then . . .
WHAM
it attacks from a new direction,
I didn't expect.
What do I learn?
I get up quicker
keep moving
I learn to live in a new way
vividly aware of my wolf
and
helping others to see and live with theirs,
because,
I can look them in the eye
and tell them
I don't know their wolf
but
I know about wolves.

Cindy Mitchell Perkins

Flashing Back
(April 1995)

I sit
in therapy
talking about one hard piece
of the reality
the finality
of my life now.
Then Suddenly
the sirens and noise start
I stare at my hands
wanting there to be a
tiny hand to hold once again
Then the sirens
slice through
my innermost being
They cut and rip
I cringe
I can't turn off the noise
Sirens
People moving
"We're gonna get you out of here,"
some man says
"I don't care," is how I feel
"Help my Heidi"
The noise.
It surrounds me
I hear another voice
a familiar safe voice

I fight to reach it.
Like swimming out of deep, deep water
holding my breath
the voice says to move to make eye contact
I want to

Keeping Heidi Close

I'm trying
Why is it so hard?
I finally make contact
with my therapist
I have finally returned from my trip
back to the trauma of
June tenth
Or have I?
I'm still fighting to be back
Now—a day later
I still feel like there are two parts of me
one here and one still back with the noise.

Paradox—My Life

One huge paradox
Joy—I used to feel
Emptiness and Grief—I feel now
Glad Heidi is okay
Glad I have a faith that
helps me know that.

Mad—that she's not here to hold
and be okay in my arms.
Warm feelings—being cared about
and supported
Wish—that people didn't have to
half smile—as a plaque is placed
at the softball field in her memory
Heidi Tobiason Softball Field
Cry—because there is a plaque
Smile—as her friends play ball
Cry—because Heidi can't

We all were at Irish Point Beach on our beloved Swans Island, flying kites in Heidi's memory in May of 1995, what is now our family of three, and some very special people in our lives. We went off to Swans Island to go to the quarry and find a special stone to become her memorial stone. Ultimately it was all the kids who all agreed on the beautiful stone defined by Erik as perfect, because it was pink. Heidi loved pink and the stone was shaped like a mountain, which is where Camp Calumet is and she loved that too. A special thank you to Erik, Hans, Anders, Curt, Suz, Chelsea, and Amy. And to all the adults who helped load it so it could come home to live in Yarmouth.

Irish Point Beach
(1995)

Walking to the edge of Irish Point Beach
I came upon a small stream winding its way down to the ocean
I was reminded quietly of your life.

The still pond up in the marsh . . .
your quiet beginning, with still eyes
and peaceful acceptance of your new world.

The stream trickled smoothly downhill
over the smooth sand of the beach
those first few magical years that were so smooth for you
easy-going acceptance of everyone . . .
healthy protected cocoon that you lived in.

The stream dug deeper into the sand,
carving its own direction
you becoming your own person
carving your own path.

The stream spread out becoming thinner but wider . . .
laughing . . . bubbling. . . .

The stream went over and around bumps,
some small sandy ones, some bigger rocky ones.
You, in your beginning adolescence,
finding the bumps, big and small, but in your easy way, like the stream
going over and around them, while staying
together hanging onto you.

The stream spread out to encompass
the whole beach
your arms spread out to love so many.

The stream slides into the ocean to
become a part of the bigger whole,
to be connected to it all. . . .
You slide into the ocean to become part of the bigger whole,
to be connected to us all

The Rock
(June 1995)

The rock has many paths
they all reach the peak
which holds a cross.

My journey has taken many paths
none of which reaches the goal I want.
My path has crossed many others
as do the paths on the rock.

No matter how much I try, I keep
hitting walls in my journey
that block my way.
I can't get where I want.
I can't have what I want.

I climbed the rock
I chose a path
it was difficult . . . scary . . . steep
It had many obstacles . . .
I crawled and inched through them.
I came to a wall
that blocked my way.
I couldn't get where I wanted
I couldn't have what I wanted.
I didn't know what it was about the rock
that I needed and couldn't get to.
I haven't known what it was that I was

reaching for all year.
The rock taught me.
I wanted Heidi.
I couldn't get to her
just as I couldn't get to the
cross at the top of the rock.

They were both just out of my reach.

When I recognized the cross
that I couldn't reach,
I no longer needed to reach it.
I knew I held it.

When I recognized that Heidi
was what I needed to reach
I was able to say goodbye,
feel my grief,
and hold her in the only way I now can . . .
in my heart.

(Written after returning from a short unexpected trip to Sedona, as described in an entry in the Journals section, where I tried to reach the top of Cathedral Rock.)

One Year
(June 10, 1995)

A year!!!!
How can it be.
Heidi has been
gone for a year.
I have somehow
survived a year of grieving.
I have gotten through all
the days that
the year brought!
I dreaded this day.
In some ways I also
thought
somehow it was a finish line.
I had done it. Done the year
all the anniversaries and
holidays
all the moments she
wasn't beside me.

Phew
a relief
somehow I had gotten through
this year
so now
I know how to do this. . . .

Yet . . .
now as I step into year two

I realize I have to
do it all over again.
Some parts will be familiar
will never change.

She will somehow stay eleven.
Hans will grow and change.
We will all grow and change
her friends too
our memories of her will keep her eleven
while the rest of the world
goes on.
Lives on.

I live the moments of the accident
over and over
especially at this anniversary time.
As if . . .
I can create a different story
As if . . .
by redoing it
I get to look in the rearview mirror
see the truck
get out of the way.
And go merrily
off to swimming lessons,
as we planned.
As if. . .
As if . . .
As if . . .

Hello
(June 15, 1995)

Hello my Heidi
this is new for me.
I have always believed that your spirit lived on.
Now I know and feel it
I have to learn how to live
with that part of you.

The joy in knowing that
feels so complete.
It is matched only by
the pain in saying goodbye
to you the way I have
known you for eleven years.

I felt you in the wind at the Grand Canyon
I saw you in the star at Oak Creek
I recognized you in the falling star at Swans Island
the rainbow at Heidi's field the day of dedication and Calumet last
summer
So are you following me around or what?

It feels like you are
It feels like I am wrapped up in your love right now.
Maybe that's why I like the "Wrap Me in a Rainbow" song.
You're my rainbow.
Wrap your colors, light and wind around me.

I read your writing and am so thankful that I have that.
Your photos are still too hard for me to find joy in.
But your writing brings me that sometimes
sometimes it brings tears

Stay with me, Heidi
Help me to remember that you are still here in this new way
through much more than just my memories
The way you touch others' lives still
the wind, rainbows and stars
through the love that
you shared with
all.
I love you,
mom

Goodbye
(June 15, 1995)

I said goodbye to you at the Grand Canyon
What does that mean?
It means I felt you there wrapped around me
in the wind and so could say
goodbye to the you that I have been
trying to hang onto.

That you is the you whom I feel when I walk
into your room.
And look at all your treasures
left untouched by you for a year now.

Goodbye to the trumpet singing
noisily through our home.
goodbye to the puppet that you created
and the imagination that lived with it
Goodbye to school projects that
you dove into so intensely.

Goodbye to hugging you at bed time
and waking you up with a hug in the morning
Goodbye to sitting in your room and sharing
stories and accomplishments

Goodbye to excitement about new clothes
and attachments to old ones.
Goodbye to the softball team
and the class of 2001.

Goodbye to that casual circle
of friends whom I would meet
at school functions because
they were your friends' moms.

Goodbye to your laughter
your smiles . . . your tears . . .
your hugs . . . your frustrations . . .
being called the meanest mom in the world . . .
and the bestest mom in the world.

Goodbye to those times when I
would give you a hug
to talk you down from
a place of complete frustration and anxiety.

Goodbye to your blossoming womanhood.
Goodbye to that part of me that was blossoming with you.
Goodbye to all the hopes and dreams we shared.
Even goodbye to Nana's teacups for your children.

Goodbye Heidi, I will always love you, mom CPT

A Tiny Seed
(1995)

A miracle
grew
brought great joy
Then
WHAM!
In one moment
the pain came
the emptiness
Only the dried leaves
were left
Her beautiful life
had moved on
That happy soul
is growing somewhere else
now

I Was There
(June 10, 2005)

I was there when you were born
pink and covered in
soft . . . white . . . cream . . .
so pure . . .
so innocent . . .
so perfect. . . .
I now have an image of you . . .
white and pure . . .
somehow . . . ethereal . . .
a miracle so long waited for . . .
a miracle now . . .
still here . . . still in new ways
Eleven . . . eleven . . . eleven
eleven years I held you in my arms . . .
eleven years . . . I have now yearned to hold you in my arms. . . .
You have now been gone as long as I had you here. . . .
How can that be?
Eleven years. . . .
The First went so fast . . . so fleeting. . . .
Eleven Years
the second seem so long . . . eternal even. . . .
So long since I have held you . . .
Eleven years
How can that be?
The same yet different . . .
so different
so so different. . .

Therapy

Over time, I was slowly coming to the realization that this process of grief was not something that you graduate from. It was going to be a lifelong process. This understanding helped me develop my explanation that grief is more like a double helix that is fluid rather than linear. I was very blessed to have found the right therapist for me. She also understood that I would not finish my grief. Grief is revisited throughout your life. She was someone who understood that we hold trauma in our bodies. She was someone who asked nothing of me and everything of me. I was able to trust her enough to help me learn to live with and hold my pain. I did not need to understand why and what we were doing. I just needed to feel held and safe when I was in my therapy.

Therapy is hard work. Finding the right person for you is critical. Be sure the person you have found is someone you trust and feel safe with. At times, when I was not cognitively conscious of the depth of my pain, she would help me find it in my body and then touch the emotions that I was so wanting to stay away from. This approach at a very visceral level helped move the trauma from my body and release many stuck emotions and memories. Known as Somatic Experiencing, this technique is proven to be very effective for trauma work. It was developed by Dr. Peter Levine. I'm not sure where I would be today had I not found my therapist, Stephanie.

Therapy also takes time. I went to weekly sessions two hours from my home for most of seven years. I learned and grew in many ways. I believe I found someone inside me, who had been there all the time but had gotten stuck and shut down much earlier in my life. This part of me closed off again when Heidi died. But it came alive again through the work I did in therapy. It also brought back the knowledge that every moment of our lives counts and we must fully live it. I found strength, in this process, to become who I wanted to be. I made choices to reach deep inside and trust myself. I found that person inside me, whom I hadn't dared to let out many years ago.

Most sessions would begin with me carefully scanning my body for any place that felt tight or knotted up, or maybe just noticing that part of my body. Sometimes, I was not even sure why I was noticing such a spot. She would help me focus on that place in my body. It was very important that I remained grounded (feet on the ground) and in visual connection with her. The emotions I would feel could overwhelm me easily, but I would stay focused on the feeling in my body and look to Stephanie for support.

Her comforting looks through eye contact would reassure me to stay with that part of my body and the feeling that was there, no matter how difficult. Her eye contact reminded me without words that I was not alone. She was holding my pain with me. We would explore together the color, temperature, and feelings within that place in my body. Breathing into that part of my body while visualizing the color or the temperature would often bring up images or feelings or both. I did not always know what the feelings were about or even why they were so strong, but, learning to stay with them and not run away, I was often able to hold the intensity and then ultimately release them from that part of my body. There were days when I could then verbalize what they might be about, often through a clear visualization that had come up during this body experience. By the time my sessions were over, I was usually exhausted but also relieved. After walking around a little bit in the fresh air, as Stephanie suggested, a feeling of being energized and renewed would often be the result.

The insights from the sessions would come later. The healing took many years. Sometimes, I would feel as if something was totally healed, as if I had had a "light bulb" moment and some part of my journey was now totally understood. I think now that this realization is more about understanding for that moment in time. I'm not sure that anything in our lives is ever totally understood. After all, this journey we are on takes a lifetime and we are always learning and growing. Grief and trauma work the same way. What makes sense one moment, day, week, year, or decade even, may come to a completely different understanding and revelation sometime later in our lives.

Different people, experiences, and insights come and go in our lives and, if we are open to them, we will grow and learn from each one of them. We have to be open in order to have these experiences. I have tried in my life's journey to be open to new experiences and even things I don't understand. I believe that losing Heidi resulted in large part in my ability to let go of the belief that I knew all the answers. I was forced to realize that I did not have control. I did not know everything. Not even close!

I had to take in and let go of the illusion that, if I just did everything right, then bad things would not happen to me. I could somehow control and keep my children safe. If only. . . .

This realization was something that I had to remind myself of constantly in order to parent Hans in a way that was fair to his growing into and becoming his own person. I really wanted to put him in a bubble and never let him out. Now, he is in his thirties and there are still times when I want to do that. He would not have become the wonderful, independent man that he now is, if I had covered him in bubble wrap. I know there were times when I protected him more than I might have and other times I let go, but not without inner turmoil and struggle. Reminding myself I was not in control was a regular conversation with myself.

Year two and on is when I was able to believe that life was too short not to live it. For probably the first time in my life, I became truly conscious of decisions I made and of my own happiness. I moved consciously through more of life's choices instead of letting them happen to me when possible. That sentence in itself is an oxymoron. If we do not have control, then, don't we have to just let life happen?

When we are at a crossroad, we can go right, left, back, straight, or stand still. The direction we choose has an impact on everything else. Yet, the unknown and events that are out of our control are still possible. My decision is to pick a direction, knowing I made a choice and understanding that, even in choice, I do not have full control of the events.

On June 10, 1994, I chose to go through that tollbooth. I could have taken a different direction. For a very long time, I tortured myself, rehashing the wish, "if only I had taken the other road." The inevitable conclusion was that Heidi would still be alive. I wanted to recreate that road, that decision. I could not. The truth is, I don't know what would have happened if I'd gone in a different direction. I don't get to know. That is what happened that day. That's all I know. I will never know the outcomes for all the other possible scenarios I come up with.

Some people might at some point in their lives think, "What if I hadn't moved to that town? I would not have met my best friend. I would not have met my partner." Maybe or maybe not. Those are the choices we made at the time. The choices we make consciously, we know, in the moment to be the best ones. Looking back, they may or may not turn out to be the ones that were best for us, because we have no control over long-term outcomes. I have never forgotten that many of the moments in time when my mind went to "but," or "what if?," or "if only," I ended up realizing, were my way of wanting the outcome to be different. I still go there sometimes and still hear my therapist Stephanie's voice remind me that the outcome will still be the same. "As if. . . ." That short phrase brings me back to the present and the choice that I made that cannot be changed.

I learned that in order to take care of others, Hans especially, I had to take care of myself. If you are not taking care of yourself, you will have nothing left to give those who you love the most. I also learned that I did not have to do it all. I accepted help from others which, as a caretaker myself, was not easy at first. Someone early on reminded me how honored I am when I can help someone else and that the same is true for others helping me.

I learned to trust myself. I found out that I have good instincts and learned to believe in myself. I discovered that I could move forward. Stephanie likened learning to trust yourself to writing a paper. You can get overwhelmed with the topic or expected length. If you just take that first step and trust that you can do it, you find yourself moving forward. She called this, trusting your process. When you are slugging through each day trying to figure out how to go on, trusting the process—your process—seems like the biggest mountain you could ever climb. Sometimes the process feels overwhelming. You get stuck on questions like: What is my professor wanting from this? Why do they need forty pages? How can I possibly say all I need to say in five pages?

Getting started is too hard. Getting through the day is overwhelming. The mantra of one step at a time is important to remember, here. When I do trust myself to pay attention to whatever feelings are happening in that moment, I find unexpected relief in that. Another positive outcome of learning to trust myself was to experience moments, or days even, of feeling like myself again or maybe discovering my new self. Acknowledging to yourself that this journey in your life doesn't have a map enables you to begin walking in the direction that feels right for you. I hope you will feel empowered when you begin trusting yourself to take steps forward, as I did.

The time period between Christmas 1994 and the first anniversary of Heidi's loss, June 10, 1995, was a period of deep soul searching for me. I was in intense therapy—weekly—and I was in a grad school program that involved looking at yourself, your feelings, and your process. Reading over my many journal entries, I am amazed at how many ways I was growing during this time. My conscious awareness of myself, my life, my childhood, who I was, and who I was to become was spiraling around me daily. I was looking at who I was and was becoming, more and more conscious about who I wanted to be.

Opportunities were presenting themselves regularly for me to look at myself and learn and grow. I had a choice to jump in or ignore and walk away. I jumped in. After all, embracing learning opportunities was something I had learned from Heidi. When I started grad school, I entered into my Masters in Counseling program with a very different attitude than I had when I went through all my earlier education. In grad school, I was driven to learn everything I could. Before I went to the first class, I decided to volunteer at every opportunity, so that I could learn and experience everything that was available for me. I believed strongly that I had to know myself well, to be available to help others.

The personal drive and growth I brought to graduate school carried through into my life after Heidi died. This desire to know myself became critical as I looked at, felt, and learned to trust my feelings each day. I brought them to consciousness through talking, writing, drawing, crying, being angry, and meditating.

I tried not only to understand my feelings, but also those of Hans and David. I was very aware we were all walking this path differently, each in our own way. Trusting your own process, and the process of those around you is a big task. As I worked through my own grief, I was also learning how to be a mother to a young child who had lost his beloved sibling. My child has his own trauma and memory of the day his sibling died, and these are different from mine. They always will be. So, I listened, watched, and learned about children and grief, which led me to understand that children are little Buddhas. They know how to be in the moment. They have their grief, sadness, madness, in the many forms that takes, and then they smile and go play. We, the adults, have so much to learn from them. Hans was and is still one of my greatest teachers in this respect and so many others.

Stephanie would also gently challenge me to think about something differently and often a well-timed question would bring up very strong feelings. I could get very angry with her, though also eventually would pay attention to what she was suggesting. I knew I was safe enough with her to do both. For example, she asked whether maybe I was hanging onto my spiritual experience of June 10 so strongly that I would not have to go to the depths of my grief. First, I was angry that she would question that. I looked into her eyes and saw compassion and support. Because I saw that familiar caring, I started to cry. I cried that day in a way that I had not allowed myself to do. I went to the depth of my grief and found that I could hold it and still hold onto my spiritual experiences and belief even and especially while sitting in my grief. They were both true.

Many of my personal insights were initiated in those long hard sessions in Stephanie's office. I drove from Maine to Massachusetts weekly all those years, because I had found a person whom I was able to trust enough to walk with me into the depth of my pain and grief. I found a person whom I did not have to take care of one hour each week. She challenged me with compassionate care to hold my grief and be able to participate in my life. My gratitude to her goes beyond words. My wish for each of you is that you find your "Stephanie" to walk with you into and through the depths of your grief.

SPIRITUALITY

Spirituality is the circuitous route we all take individually to find our own beliefs. For me, this journey included a multitude of paths through organized religion, nature, spirituality, and my own exploration with openness to new experiences. My spiritual journey has been braided tightly with my journey of grief. I believe that we each have our own spiritual journey here on earth. We are all in different places with our beliefs. There is a reason why there are so many approaches to faith, religion, and spirituality in the world. Each one has something to offer someone.

Our spiritual journey is our human attempt to make sense of a realm that we cannot see. We try to figure out how to make sense of our existence here and our relationship to the spiritual realm. These journeys are very personal. We all have to find our way and hold onto what works and let go of what does not work for us. We look to sources that speak to us such as organized religion, spirituality, science, and nature. As human beings, we often look for a community of people with similar values.

Losing your child will challenge you to look at, question, and redefine your beliefs. You can choose to accept this challenge or not. My choice was to accept it. My grief pushed me to grapple with my faith, beliefs, and all that I had grounded myself in, prior to losing Heidi. My spirituality and faith have been a huge part of this journey for me. A community of people with a faith is one of the highest priorities in my life. My spiritual communities have been my foundation. I have been a member of many denominations during my lifetime and currently am a member of three spiritual communities, two of which are churches. I still belong to my tiny little non-denominational church on the island where I lived for seven years. I still hold my membership at the United Church of Christ (UCC) congregation in the town where I raised my children, because it feels like my home base. I am very active in the Lutheran Church through Camp Calumet Lutheran, a spiritual home for me since 1967. I don't know what I would have done without my faith and these communities.

I grew up in the 50s and 60s, with protestant Sunday school and church. My mother made sure we attended with some regularity. Her strong faith and that of my grandmother and great-grandmother formed my foundational beliefs. I watched all of them turn to the pages of their bibles for comfort and answers when they were struggling. All three of these women had also lost a child. (I wish I could go back and talk to them now—oh, the conversations I imagine we would have).

Sunday school was a given throughout my childhood. It was something you did. My father did not go to church. When I asked why he didn't have to go to church and I had to go to Sunday school, he said that he had served his time, as if it was something you did as a kid and grew out of. That framing also implied to me that it was a punishment of sort. There was a period of time when I thought that to be true. I looked forward to when Sunday would be the day when I could do what I wanted and not go to Sunday school. He saw church as something you did because you were supposed to and, thus, so did I as a growing child. I am grateful to have found and held onto my faith, which continues to grow and change as I age. The balance of my parents opposite relationships to faith helped me to look at and question more than I might have, had they been more in line with each other. The mixed messages I received gave me permission to ask "why do we go to church?" What do I believe? I have done both—attended regularly and taken breaks from attending an organized service, yet never have stopped developing my own faith.

The friends I have found at church, as well as the rituals and prayers, comfort me. Christmas Eve candlelight services still bring comfort to me, as they did when I was a child, when my mother and I would attend, in the quiet of the night. Back then, we would try to carry our lit candles all the way home. Now, you have to return candles after blowing them out. So, on the way back, I always imagine the candle glowing until I get home. In the midst of Covid 19 isolation and virtual Christmas Eve services, I had my candle at home and kept it lit, as I sat quietly, even after the service was over. This reminder of a long-held tradition has been calming and reassuring especially during the years since Heidi passed. Every year, when I visit her grave after this service, I relight a candle with her. In this way, I keep this tradition alive with her.

Our family was not committed to one particular religion. One Easter Sunday, there was a blizzard where we lived, and we could not get to the Congregational Church across town, where we had always gone—the church of my mother's family. My mother mentioned that a new church had been built at the end of our street, and suggested we could walk there. Walk we did, through the storm and into the brand-new Lutheran Church that would become our spiritual home for the next three years. I was confirmed in that church and learned that, for me, a community of people with similar values and a safe place to talk about my questions and beliefs was the most important part in choosing my church.

At the end of eighth grade, the day I was confirmed, we moved to another town and another state. This move was very difficult for me. I went—resisting all the way. I was the stereotype of a very angry adolescent, refusing to participate in activities that I might have enjoyed. I realize now that my fear of such a big shift and needing to make new friends at that awkward 13-year-old age is what drove my behavior.

In my generation, most parents did not talk to children about these changes. We certainly did not talk about our feelings in my family. For me, to be aware of, and then acknowledge that I was scared to make new friends was unheard of. You were supposed to just do whatever you were told to do.

There was no Lutheran church in our new town, so, I found myself in the UCC community again. I no longer had to attend Sunday school, because there was nothing for us high schoolers, until later, when a new minister came and a youth group was started. My mother attended services frequently, and I would attend with her by choice—even though I had imagined choosing never to go again. I held strong in my refusals to accept this new place. My parents made many suggestions and I sometimes went begrudgingly, but did not allow myself to enjoy them. After a year or more of mostly resisting, I finally allowed myself to join some groups that fit for me.

At this point, a choice I made to go in a spiritual direction changed the course of my life. Journaling, listening to music, and sharing with trusted friends became lifelong habits that I developed then and have carried me through my hardest times. These tools became part of my survival mechanisms and provided the ability to keep going while learning to live with the loss of Heidi.

The decision I made to follow a spiritual path involved two groups that laid the foundation for my adult faith and became my lifeline. These communities, my high school youth group and Camp Calumet, consisted of groups of adults and kids who were accepting of who I was and provided safe environments in which to explore, question, and develop my faith. I often suggest to my clients or others that they find their own safe place in which to grieve and explore their spirituality. For me, it began at these two places. For you, it might be your church or a coffee group, yoga group, or a bereaved parents' group. The important part is that you have people you trust with whom to explore and grieve. It might be a specific place or just one or two friends that you trust.

The first of these two groups was a drop-in youth group our church organized. At the urging of my mother, I ultimately attended the group and allowed myself to have friends in this new community. Several of the people from that group remain dear friends five decades later, including one of the leaders who is now approaching 90 years of age.

We went on retreats regularly to a lodge in Jackson, New Hampshire. Set high in the White Mountains, this beautiful place, with its wrap-around porch, a fieldstone fireplace, filled with the joyful energy of young energetic teens, became my lifeline and brought me back to myself. On the front lawn, often, one or two of us could be found sitting on a giant rock and gazing out at the mountains. Rituals were developed that became organic to our group. We always were given time to work on a project. The retreat lodge required work and we enthusiastically embraced the needed tasks. An hour of quiet meditative time each day was part of our ritual. We might walk, write, sit, or read thoughts to be shared during the evening candlelight services in the little chapel that sat next to the lodge. Those services created by us teens in the 60s were so often where deep sharing of feelings and thought-provoking conversations were started.

The second of the two groups pivotal in my spiritual maturing and another rich part of my spiritual development was a Lutheran church camp that my mother had discovered. I agreed to attend it for a week, before my junior year of high school. I had refused to join the year before, because she had suggested it and it was not my idea. By the next year, I had decided that maybe a week with other kids at this camp would be a welcome break from working at my dad's pharmacy. Indeed, it was. That church camp was Camp Calumet Lutheran. Camp Calumet became, for me, an extension of the youth group retreats. It remains the center of my spiritual world, because I can count on that community to have meaningful honest conversations about anything, but most especially my faith. Calumet has consistently been where I can look deeply at my faith, sometimes strengthening my beliefs, supporting someone else through their growth, and other times leaving me to ponder a new insight.

At Calumet in 1968, we were led through similar rituals as in my high school youth group retreats, in addition to designing and writing parts of the church services, singing camp songs and going on wonderful hiking adventures in the wilderness of the New Hampshire White Mountains. Hiking became another lifelong meditative and profoundly restorative practice for me. Hiking in the woods has always brought me calm and balance. During my 60s, I took to running, which offers me the same meditative experience.

The summer before Heidi died was my first summer as an adult staff member at Camp Calumet. I agreed to work there because Heidi wanted so badly to spend the summer there and be a staff kid. Hans was his happiest self being free to roam around camp. I am so glad that I made that decision before she died. My son, Hans, also returned to work there in his 20s and I saw that relaxed, happy being I had known as a camper many years before. He met his now wife there, that summer, and in the fall of 2020 they were married on the shores of Lake Ossipee at Camp Calumet.

I was on a spiritual journey of my own that summer of 1993. I was waiting to start my Master's Program in Clinical Psychology so had time to read, and I did. I read and absorbed every spiritual book I could get my hands on. In that community, there were many people to talk to about these readings, and with whom to question and examine my faith. During staff week, another adult staff member, Susan, who was in seminary, noticed the Matthew Fox book, *Original Blessing*,[1] that I was reading.. She commented that we should talk, since we seemed to be reading the same books. We found a bookstore nearby that carried a large variety of spiritual books for only two to five dollars. We would coordinate schedules so that we could run to the bookstore on a break and grab new books. We would absorb these books and have many late-night conversations about them before we went off to get our next set. Needless to say, we became fast friends, reading, learning, and exploring our faith together.

Throughout the summer, I explored many questions of my own faith. I looked at the Bible in ways I had never thought of. I explored stories from the woman's perspective. I read the Gnostic Gospels[2] and the Gospels of Mary[3] and Thomas[4], sections that had not been chosen to be included in the traditional version of the Bible.

I found the Gospel of Mary to be especially comforting because I was exploring who I was as a woman of faith. Mary continues to give me comfort and reassurance from the many spiritual messages my mother used to receive and the ones I get. I had not even known that these Gospels existed until that summer. Many biblical messages include

---

1 Fox, Matthew, *Original Blessing*, TarcherPerigee, 2000.

2 Payton, Jeremy, *The Gnostic Gospels Master Collection*, Mindsparkpress LTD, 2023.

3 Leloup, Jean-Yves et al., *The Gospel of Mary Magdalene*, Inner Traditions, 2002.

4 Leloup, Jean-Yves, *The Gospel of Thomas*, Inner Traditions, 2005.

visions, but Mary's messages and visions particularly resonate with me. There is an authority in her language and messages that have often validated my experiences when I receive communications from Heidi.

By the end of that summer, I was moving toward a comfortable place with my faith, beliefs, and spirituality. I was back in touch with my faith in a way that I had not been for at least a decade. I was hearing different interpretations of the Bible that made sense to me. I heard that "Love thy Neighbor," for instance could mean more than I had learned, growing up, which was that you must love everyone else; you must take care of them no matter what. According to my newer understanding, the expression advised to "love thy neighbor as thyself." Oh, I realized and came to believe, I must love myself, so that I can love my neighbor in this same and pure way. I also came to believe I must love myself so that others can love me. I have made sure to share this insight many times, over the years, with clients and friends. Love yourselves, grieving parents, love yourselves.

I wonder now, why this journey? Why this particular timing? Looking back, it begs the question of whether I was preparing for what was to come. Did something or someone in this vast universe understand more than I? I don't believe it is as simple as that. I don't have words to explain that to you. For me, "it just is." At the same time, I do not believe in coincidence.

Questions like these are lifetime explorations for me and many others. What I know and trust is that, in the summer of 1993 (a year before Heidi died), I was truly on a personal spiritual journey. My thirst to read, learn, and process all things spiritual became my focus that year. The important insights described above strengthened my faith. They also ultimately provided me with hope and the ability to be open to getting to know Heidi spiritually. I had to forgive myself—a very difficult part of my journey. I was, after all, the driver of the car in which my daughter lost her life. In order to forgive myself and find a way to move forward, I had to believe there was a much bigger reason and purpose to her death that I did not get to understand. I still do not.

I don't understand why so many young children are dying world-wide. I do believe their lives had a bigger purpose, as I believe Heidi's did—even though I don't get to know what that purpose is. She lived her life in eleven years, for that was her life here. In other words, she did the work of her lifetime in her short eleven years. This understanding leads me to the realization that I was not responsible for ending her life because she had finished her life's work. Her purpose and messages carry on in many ways in the hearts of those whose lives she touched. It was not the life I envisioned for her. The premature end of an offspring's life is never what any parent envisions for their child.

It is not in our plans, as parents, for our children to die before us. We plan to watch them grow to adulthood. We expect to embrace their decisions about schools and learning, and delight in every moment. I expected to be holding Heidi's children in my arms by now, and loving them as nanas do. I hold in my arms the children of her friends and cousins and feel incredibly blessed to be in their lives. I hold in my arms each precious one joyfully, while being painfully aware that I will never know her children.

What I remember of those moments when I lost my firstborn and only daughter has caused me to struggle with my hope and faith and, at the same time, hang on tight. Over these many years, I have had to learn to live with the excruciating pain of losing her. I have been forced to learn to hold this indescribable pain.

I remember the singing and fun in the van as we approached the toll booth. I remember the loud, excruciating CRASH. This sound will haunt me for the rest of my life. I remember seeing her on the ground and me screaming for someone to help her. The visual flash of this moment comes into my brain like a horror movie when I least expect it. So terrifying! . . . So excruciating! . . . In another visual flash that comes back repeatedly, I see the truck driver who caused this horrible scene looking down from his truck on what he had done.

After the collision, I was transported somewhere else, and thus no longer at the scene of the accident. I have spent many years reviewing this moment and my experience. Over the years, I have come to absorb what I believe was happening then and put it together with occurrences that I have experienced since then, as you will see in this section.

That memory of being with Heidi as she walked away, hand in hand with two people whom she and we all loved, continues to be clear and powerful. Many people have described bright lights, when they have had near-death experiences. I remember a bright light shining over Heidi's friend Rebecca and my son Hans, as I looked down on them as if I were above them. I had the certain knowledge that they were OK. I remember the bright light that Heidi was walking into, but also an intense illumination of all three of them. I had never thought of this experience as near-death for me because it never occurred to me that I might have been dying. I knew I was staying here. Most recently, I am starting to wonder if the "we have a pulse," I heard while in the ambulance was about me, not Heidi. I have no memory of being removed from the car or put in an ambulance. Those words seem to be my first memory after hearing David's voice.

I felt like I walked with Heidi and then watched her walk on with loved ones. I remain clear that I was giving birth to her a second time. Over the years, I have come to believe that the vision of Hans with Rebecca off to the side and my certainty that they were OK was a strong message. After seeing Heidi off, I was returning to Hans and to the rest of my life. That experience has taken many years to accept as fully as I can and, at the same time, with absolute certainty, know it to be true from the moment it happened.

Hans's strength pulled me back from the brink of death a second time in 2018, as I fought off sepsis in the ICU. My body wrapped in layers of heated blankets started to shake dramatically. I was terrified. I could not get warm. Nurses were piling more heated blankets on me. I asked Hans to hold me. His loving embrace in one terrifying moment pulled me back, as if I had been falling and he had thrown a lifeline. He did. I caught the lifeline—his love—and here I am.

I am so thankful that Hans's love, energy, and our strong spiritual connection pulled me to stay alive and living AND so profoundly sad that he has been in the position, now twice, to pull me back from the brink of death. As his parent, I wish he could have stayed in his childhood bubble of joy for many more years, instead of being thrown into these tragic realities of life so young. Being a surviving sibling is an incredible burden. Our children take this on in many ways, yet most feel an intense pressure to fill the void of the lost sibling for their parents. They often try to be everything they imagine the lost sibling would have become. What intense pressure for a child to be under!

There are many accounts of near-death experiences and almost all describe a calm, a peacefulness, and a bright light. No one has described it any better than Betty Eadie in her book, *Embraced by the Light*.[5] Reading her book validated my experience at a visceral level. I have read and absorbed her descriptions many times with an understanding deep within me that what she describes is very similar to my experience of watching Heidi walk off hand in hand with two beloved souls.

Even though I know in my soul that what I saw, experienced, and remember is true, that calm, peaceful assurance does not take away the pain of losing Heidi. Over time, that experience has helped me be sure of my new relationship with her. In those days and months after the tragedy, I woke up repeatedly with the sudden realization that it was true, she had died. She would not be coming back. It was like waking to someone hitting you over the head and knocking you down as you start to open your eyes, every day. It took months and even years to really embrace my spiritual truth about her, because that meant she was really gone with all the hopes and dreams we parents have for our children. Yet, at the same time as I struggled with all this and cried and fought with my grief, I also had an indescribable peacefulness in my heart, an absolute knowledge, if you will. The irony is that I had to embrace my grief to fully sit in my peaceful self. My sense of peace and my grieving self are both part of who I am.

Heidi's loving Aunt Louise had died three years before Heidi died. When she was only in second grade, Heidi had written and read a story for Aunt Louise's memorial service. Years later, she had told her friend

---

5 Eadie, Betty, *Embraced by the Light*, Gold Leaf Press, 1992.

that she would not be afraid to die because she would be with Aunt Louise, her namesake, Heidi Louise. What fifth grader has that kind of conversation? WHY?

I was with Heidi. I know I was at her birth—her birth into the next part of her life. I stood and looked on as my little girl held the hands of Louise and Bill and walked into the light. "For where two or three are gathered in my name, there am I in the midst of them." (*Matthew 18:20 RSV*) comes to mind. A newer translation is offered in *The Message, The Bible in Contemporary Language,*[6] "when two or three of you are together because of me, you can be sure that I'll be there." I am very sure that she and all of us were in the presence of holiness and surrounded by love that would protect her and us. Why else would I have felt and seen what I did? She moved on to another plane at the tender and wise age of eleven.

She moved to a place that I call Heaven. Others have different names for this place. These names are not important. Call that place what you need to and what you are comfortable with, but know that your child is in this safe, warm, well-lit place that I call Heaven and you call whatever is comforting to you. I hope you are able to find a way of knowing your child is somewhere that is safe and warm. I know not why. You know not why. I don't like it. On good days, I find comfort in this memory and my knowledge. On not so good days, I just simply want her here with me. As the years go by, more of my days are those good days filled with certainty.

The image of the doctor standing by my bedside does not go away. I knew by his face. "We tried; we did all we could." These empty words came from someone who wanted to be bringing much different news. There are the tears forming in my eyes, now as I write this, thinking of that moment I could not change. I hurt beyond words and would need time, in that depth of darkness, in order to hang onto the many hopeful messages I have been given over time (Heidi walking off, orbs, messages through Maryann, etc.).

---

6 Peterson, Eugene H. (translator), *The Bible in Contemporary Language,* NavPress, 2005.

On days of lost hope, I find despair because my precious Heidi is not with me. Yes, I still have those—though not as often as in the beginning. She is not 36 or more years old, as I would wish, and coming by tomorrow to celebrate Thanksgiving Day and watch the parade as we enjoyed doing when she was young. And yet she will be here with me as she is every day. I will watch for signs of her, as I have learned to do. She truly is in the sun, wind, stars, and rainbows of this and another world. I know many think that this sounds trite. For me, it is real and my lifeline. I have had many experiences where my body has a physical reaction (chills or a feeling of energy passing through me), or tears come when I look up and see that rainbow, feel the wind, or take a photo and find an orb right there in my photo, and sometimes even with my naked eye. I just have to look and be open. I believe she is doing much more important things. I have to believe there is a reason. There's got to be a reason I don't yet understand, so, for the rest of my life, I will keep looking up and searching for that reason. I have reached deep inside and found my faith. I questioned and fought with my faith. I have chosen to believe. I believe she is well and has continued to live on in her new way. I have to believe this. You will believe what you want and need. You will question and argue. I hope you are able to find something to believe in. Find a way to believe in your child and your connection. For me, it was too hard to believe she just stopped existing.

As so well said in Cidny Bullens's song, written after the loss of his daughter, "I Gotta Believe in Something." That song, from his 1999's award-winning album *Somewhere Between Heaven and Earth*[7], was written and recorded in the first two years after the death of (then) Cidny's eleven-year-old daughter, Jessie. As I played this song over and over again, its message resonated with me. I gotta believe in something! I could not imagine not having something to believe in. My believing is what I held onto and that album and this song by Cidny let me know I was not alone.

7 Bullens, Cidny, "I Gotta Believe in Something", *Somewhere Between Heaven and Earth*, Mommy's Geetar Music/BMI, 1999.

My experience has shown me that she is not gone completely. She is gone from this plane and the day-to-day life I had imagined for her. She lives on in her new way and I feel blessed that I have the gift of paying attention and knowing she is very much OK in her way. I want to be clear. I do not like that she is not here as I want her to be. My choice would be for her to be here. I did not get to choose. I hold both my wish for her to be here and the comfort of knowing that she is OK in her new way.

Learning to live with multiple truths has been a long and confusing journey. Christmas Eve, when I always visit her grave, is one of those times when the multiple truths hit me. I stand by her gravestone, which reads, "Do not stand by my grave and weep. I am not here. I do not sleep." As I sob each year and then wipe the tears, I am profoundly aware of the irony. I walk away determined to remember this message, since I truly believe she does not sleep, even though my pain and grief are ever present.

My friend Abby suggested we go to her grave the first year at midnight after church, in the pouring rain. Of course, we went. We cried. We were walking back to the car when a police car pulled in. My dear friend firmly told the young officers who I was and that I needed to be there, so they should leave us alone. They did, and now, it is my tradition! Thank you, Abby

I am thankful that the spiritual experience of June 10, 1994, my ability and decision to pay attention to that experience and many others, along with my foundation in my faith, have helped me to be in my life since that day.

Decisions / Choices

Our lives are filled with decisions and choices we have made. Some decisions we are happy with, others we second-guess and wish we could change, even though we know we can never go back and change them. The topic of decisions has loomed large in my life since Heidi's death. My guilt led me to wanting to have made different decisions. I spent some three to five years after the tragedy, reliving the choices I made on June 10, 1994. Through these years, many were the times when I could get trapped in my mind, finding an easy resolution to the day, by hitting rewind and making different choices. These choices included putting reluctant Hans in the car, having Heidi change seats, using a different car, and turning away from the part of the highway where we ultimately had our accident. I finally learned through therapy that continuing to go over these decisions was fruitless and even harmful. I ultimately have accepted the futility of reliving the circumstances of my choices: no matter how many times I could revisit it all, the outcome would never change. Even now, there are days when I start to revisit those decisions and a simple thought of "as if," a reminder of the expression Stephanie, my therapist, frequently used, brings back to mind the futility of this conversation with myself.

Early on, I made a choice to be in my life with love and hope. I made choices to try to lead from my heart with love. I did not want, and chose not, to lead with my anger. There were times when it would have been easy to lead with anger. I had a lot to be angry about. I decided I did not want anger to be the driving force in dealing with my grief. Don't get me wrong, I was angry and I found ways to let my anger out.

There were times when my anger was misdirected and exploded in words and actions that hurt those whom I cared about the most. As I grew to understand these moments, I tried hard to own my hurtful actions and learn from them so I could find healthier ways to express my anger. Being honest about our anger is the first step in being able to control our angry reactions.

One decision I made was grounded in my strong feeling that I did not need the truck driver to be punished. I did not want my anger to be my most compelling resource. I know the driver did not get up that day and decide to change all of our lives by ramming his truck into our van. Maybe having the recollection of seeing him looking down on the scene he had created helped keep him human in my memory. I had two very loving sweet uncles in my life who were truck drivers. I know what it would have been like for them, if they had been the driver in an accident that took the life of anyone and most especially a child. They would have been devastated, and that truth would have been something they carried the rest of their lives. I made a choice to let the drivers' journey be his and not mine. Our tragedy was an accident and I do not need to see the driver punished. Blame and punishment for him are not going to change our outcome.

I learned that anger is a healthy emotion. I have since made sure to share this insight with my clients over the years. It is what we choose to do with our anger that is important. I work hard to live that truth and not hurt others or myself with my anger. It was frightening to allow myself to look inside and find my anger because I knew it was immense. I was scared my anger would overtake me. It seemed easier to not acknowledge that I was angry, or so it seemed to me. By honestly expressing and stating my anger, I have been able to live, leading with love and hope, at least most of the time. My decision to open the internal door to my anger and stare it down became incredibly healing for me.

Along my journey since losing my daughter, I have made many decisions. Among them was that agonizing decision, made early on, to get up! In the early days after the accident, I would wake up and for a split second, I would forget. I would think my world was the same.

Then, suddenly, before the thought had finished entering my psyche, I would realize my reality. Heidi had died. It was true. Tears would often just come and the desire to just pull the covers over my head and go back to sleep, so I wouldn't have to face another day, seemed like the best plan. Each day, I did what felt like climbing a mountain. I got up and stayed up! This was my gigantic accomplishment for much of that first year and sometimes even much later on. This decision was one of many that I am so very glad I made.

After the tears and allowing in the reality, I would next think of the day ahead, the things I would want to do on that day, and then move into the day. Most days, my snuggly little guy would come jumping into my bed for his morning snuggles and we would talk about the day and, pretty soon, the day had begun with my wonderful, in the moment, hurting and joyful (both at the same time) seven-year-old sweet boy, Hans.

Later on, I made a decision to accept (most days) what had happened and continue with my life. As I keep repeating here, this doesn't mean I like what happened. I continue to say, NO, I do not like it, nor would I have chosen it, yet, it is my reality. I had to find a way to allow this grief to be part of my life and at the same time not be the driving force of my life. The way I negotiated this dual intention has evolved over the years, in order for me to become who I am today and lead me to who I will become in the next decades of my life.

I continued to pursue my degree in Clinical Counseling. which has led to a very rewarding career in helping others. I have gained confidence in who I am in the last three decades. Most recently, I celebrated having a chapter published in *Theraplay® Innovations and Integration,*[8] a book that my colleagues, Rana Hong and A. Rand Coleman edited. This book is a collection of articles on ways to integrate various other therapeutic modalities into the Theraplay® model of therapy, which I practice and teach. My chapter, *Music, Rhythm, and the Safe and Sound*

---

8 Perkins, Cindy, "Music, Rhythm, and the Safe and Sound Protocol," *Theraplay® Innovations and Integration,* edited by Hong, Rana and Coleman, A. Rand, Jessica Kingsley Publishers, 2023, pp175-185.

Protocol, provides examples of approaches to integrate music, rhythm, and the Safe and Sound Protocol into sessions with children and their families. I explain this strategy by sharing two case studies and describing specific activities. Being part of the book release was a powerful experience for me. I was able to recognize that I had something to offer with all my esteemed colleagues and that I was, in fact, one of them. My struggle with confidence from teenage years felt like it had come full circle in that moment, because of the decision to say yes to the invitation to write that chapter.

Sometime during the pandemic, Dr. Edith Eva Eger's book, *The Choice: Embrace the Possible*,[9] was recommended to me. Dr. Eger describes her life journey and the choices she made following her deportation to Auschwitz. I found that she eloquently stated the power of choice. I have believed that power to be essential to recognize and have tried to apply it in my life since Heidi's death. She also equates our painful experiences with being gifts rather than liabilities. Both notions—the power of choice, on one hand, and painful experiences as gifts, on the other—resonated with me. I felt like Dr. Eger validated my experience. The gifts are in the insights if we choose to look and grow with them. These insights come from a changed perspective on life and what is important each day.

Tragedy can strike any of us. It dealt a blow to me that horrible day in June. I was left feeling like I had no control over my life. I did not ever want to take a risk again. Ultimately, I learned that, yes, I did not have control over what happened that particular day, yet, I had the choice every day about how I hold my pain and how I continue on in my life.

The decisions I made after the accident changed many parts of my life. I allowed myself to be who I truly was. I allowed myself to take risks, try new things and learned to speak my truth, instead of saying what I thought others wanted me to say. I realized the difference between minor inconveniences and tragedy. I have been able to move quickly away from turning small incidents or inconveniences into

9 Eger, Dr. Edith Eva , *The Choice: Embrace the Possible*, Scribner, 2017.

giant problems. I began taking on challenges that I never would have considered before, with a confidence I found deep inside me.

Another important decision was to embrace my faith. I trusted God enough to fight with him, get mad, and know that the God I believe in knows my pain and will help hold me in my most desperate moments.

I have made the decision to be open to things I do not understand. That decision has opened me up to receiving and sharing messages I have gotten from Heidi. Being open to possibilities has been the start of the realization that there is a world much bigger than any of us understand. We have to be open to listening when the bigger world communicates with us.

At the moment of her dying, I saw Heidi with her Aunt Louise and our friend Bill and the three of them walk away. This experience was and still is one of the most powerful reminders to me that there is more than us and what we can see and encounter here. I call this unfathomable dimension "another plane." Why could there not be more than we see? I don't pretend to have the answers, but I know that the openness to that other plane has brought me great peace and comfort in my hardest moments. I may not have understood right away the significance of certain occurrences, but I later came to make a decision I would not trade for the world. I ended up choosing to listen to the messages Heidi has sent me over many years through Maryann B. Russell. My intuitive friend is endowed with a beautiful gift of hearing and sharing messages from loved ones in another plane to us in this world. Her gift has brought continued communications from Heidi. One of the most powerful messages has conveyed the need to keep writing this book with Heidi and to push to get it published. Heidi's communications are so frequent and powerful that I have come to refer to Heidi's not-so-subtle reminders as ways she has to "whack" me with love to get my attention. Sometimes Maryann will get a quizzical look on her face when Heidi shows up in our session, unsure of what Heidi is insisting on expressing or why.

Most recently, it was a fun message to me. I had just purchased an electric bicycle, something I had wanted to do for several years. Until I was ready to buy one, I had decided not to go try one, because I knew I would like it but it cost too much. In an early journal entry, written not long after Heidi died, I pondered if I ever would feel the joy and freedom of bike riding again. I had found it. I had gotten the new e-bike after trying it and feeling like I was a teenager riding a beautiful bicycle again, charging uphill and downhill effortlessly and without constraints. The next day, I had an appointment with Maryann. I had woken up that morning not so much with buyer's remorse, which I might have expected because of the cost, but rather just wondering what Heidi might say. Would she be saying, "Yay, mom! Good for you, have fun!" or "Mom! What were you thinking? That's a lot of money!" I had not mentioned anything about the e-bike purchase to Maryann, so when Heidi showed up and wanted Maryann to let me know she was very happy I had gotten the bicycle, Maryann got that quizzical look. but passed on the message. I started to laugh and explained that I had wondered about Heidi's reaction, a few hours before. Heidi then kept nudging Maryann to also say she was really glad I had gotten the lobster-trap-looking carrier for the back rack of the bike. I laughed again—that part of my purchase, totally impulsive, had made me smile all the way home. Heidi wanted me to know that she would be riding in my lobster-trap carrier and I do feel nudges from time to time.

I especially felt a nudge when I was out riding on our beloved Swans Island not long after I had gotten the bike. I rode it on Swans Island in May, June, and July. I returned to the island in October and went for a ride to the Burnt Coat Harbor Lighthouse. I snapped the picture you see below, that day. I didn't notice my little green Orb-Angel in the photograph until I looked at the picture a few minutes later, and there she was, sitting in the lobster-trap carrier as she said she would be!

My Orb-Angel in her passenger seat

Cindy Mitchell Perkins

Heidi can be very direct with her messages through Maryann and, most often now, I have already received these messages myself. I find that recently, as I sit with Maryann, most often, what comes from Heidi validates messages I have already gotten.

One of the hardest decisions I made, a few years after losing Heidi, was to end my marriage of 20 years. My husband, David, and I loved each other and still do, yet, watching each other's grief and how we grieved was too hard. We became one of the many couples who were not able to stay together after the loss of a child. Our divorce became another devastating loss to all three of us. The dissolution of our marriage was certainly not what I had hoped and dreamed for my family. David and I worked hard to continue parenting Hans together with love. We still care deeply for each other and are acutely aware this was not what we had envisioned for our family. The pain and turmoil that this breakup added to my young son's life is something I will always hold deep in my soul.

Eight years ago, I made the decision to start running at 60 years old. I'm still running. After having just completed a two-day relay last weekend, it would have been easy to take a few days off or stop running. I was tired and really did not want to get up and run. But, during this race, I had made the decision to commit to this very event for five more years—after which time I would reevaluate. So, I got up, put my running gear on, and got out to run. . . Once outside, I didn't run my usual three miles, because I decided it was a five-mile day. And it was a glorious one! As I was editing this manuscript for publication, I was a few weeks away from running my ninth half marathon the day before my 71st birthday. I did run that race and came in first in my age group, which totally surprised me, and reminded me that I am capable of surprising things. The decision to keep running is one I am very proud of and glad I have stuck to.

I made the decision to be open and honest in this book. I am not trying to convince anyone to cope with grief the way I did. Each of us has to wander and search for our own path. What decisions have you made in your life? How have they affected your life? How will you use

145

those decisions to go forward? What decisions are you making today—to write, draw, walk, paint, repair a hurt relationship, sew, dance, call a friend, create something about you and see if that will help you move along your most difficult path? Every decision you make means moving forward into the moment of each day. Be conscious of your decisions. Be open to things that your brain might not be able to wrap itself around and yet your heart knows are true. For example, the decision to go through your child's belongings is a difficult one. It first means opening the door to their room and walking in. In my case, there were hidden messages within her possessions, many of which also opened up more questions for me, related to my beliefs and her life.

As you move forward in your life, please remember that you do have choices about how you take those steps forward into the rest of your life each and every day.

Heidi and her friends at her last birthday party

Hidden Messages

Heidi's Belongings

Going through your child's belongings is a task I wish on no one. Deciding to walk into your child's room is beyond words. Some days, opening the door to Heidi's room was calming. As I first entered, I felt her presence. I probably was pretending she was off at school or at a friend's house. Soon though, the tears would come as they are now, writing this, so many years later. She wasn't coming back to this space she had created. Her dollhouse, so carefully crafted by her dad and me, evoked so many memories. Her bedsheets and duvet cover, which we had carefully picked out to be green and purple, because Heidi was green and I was purple, brought a smile and then tears. I still have, cherish, and use this bedsheet set.

Over time, in Heidi's bedroom, I started to open folders and boxes, and even her trumpet case. Venturing into her room and going through her things, I often found surprising messages from her. Were the messages something she was trying to communicate, even before she died? How can that be? I don't know. I have no logical explanation for some of those communications. There is, however, an intuitive voice deep in all of our souls, that we know reveals what is true. We do not always know how or why we know; we just know. We learn to trust with experience our own sense of truth, or we ignore what our soul is trying to tell us. Each of us handles that differently. Many things that happened before and after Heidi died I know in my soul to be true. I will not defend or explain them to anyone. They just are true. I have met many people, over the years, who have shared similar experiences.

If you have had experiences of the same kind, I encourage you to trust your instinct.

In this book, I describe the messages I found, along with my reactions and beliefs about them. Since her death, I have had to learn new ways of communicating with her and keeping her close. I hope you will take from my experiences what resonates with you and embrace your own intuitions and feelings in the ways that work for you. You might say, "Oh, yes, experiences like this happen to me and I just know." You might say, "I've had similar experiences, but haven't known what to do with them." I say to you, "Trust your instincts. You do know. Believe what your heart is saying to you." These moments tore me apart and helped me move on, all at the same time.

One of the first messages I received came from a friend and then the exact same message from yet another friend. Connie, my high school youth group advisor, and Deede, Rebecca's mother, were from very different parts of my life and had never met. First, Connie called to tell me she had a visit from Heidi. She described Heidi, with feathers in her hair, visiting her at the end of her bed, during the night. At the end of Connie's bed, Heidi stood on a hope chest that wasn't part of Connie's bedroom furniture. Heidi said to Connie, "Please, tell my mother I am OK." A few months passed and Deede and I were on a walk, when Deede shared the exact same experience. Standing on the same hope chest, with feathers in her hair, Heidi was insistent again with her message to me, "Please, tell my mother I am OK". When Connie first brought me this message, I was frustrated that Heidi had not just come to me. After hearing the exact same message from Deede, I understood that I had needed to hear it from two different people, for me to fully believe this was a message, rather than just a dream I was having. It would have been very easy for me to dismiss it as my dream, because it would have been a validation of my wishes in those early days, if the experience had just been mine.

The night before Heidi died, she wrote a story that she was determined to finish. I did not understand her panic over its completion that very night. She was so very emphatic about it. There was no arguing with her. Bed time was not as important as the desperate energy she gave out about her need to finish this story that night. She just kept saying, "It HAS to be done tonight. I HAVE to finish this." Because of my teacher background, I kept asking, "when is this due?" and "Is this due tomorrow? Maybe we could ask your teacher if you could have more time." "No Mom, it's not due till next week, BUT I HAVE to finish it tonight," she would repeat, urgently.

Here is her story. Thanks go to my dear sister-in-law, her Aunt Leslie, who spent hours the day before her memorial service retyping the text and making sure it was readable. It was read at the service. I still have it included here, so her message is available to any of her friends and family members, who might need to hear that it was written with all of them in mind.

Friends Forever and Friends for Always
by Heidi Tobiason

This book is dedicated to a very dear friend of mine,
Who helped me through all the hard times,
Laughed with me through all the great ones,
Disagreed with me in all our fights.

I vividly remember the day that Jullie and I had our first fight, the one that started a trend. It was the last day of school and we were in the third grade and it was raining. So rainy that it was like a hurricane without the wind. Since it was raining we could not have our class picnic at the March's orchard, so my teacher and Mrs. Sherly decided to have a combined picnic, well, that's what the teachers called it. They opened the foldable doors that separated Mrs. Sherly's class from ours. As soon as we were free to do what we liked, I scrambled over tables and under chairs until I reached Jullie who had saved me a seat.

We ate lunch happily enough until a conversation about teachers next year was brought up. "I want Mrs. Larson, how about you?" said Jullie. I replied: "Mrs. Hill's for me, at least that's what my brother said. He had her and every teacher he said was good, was."

My brother and I have the same teachers every year, even pre-K (He was a year ahead of me, so I had the same teacher a year later), but it was just the opposite for Jullie and me. We had never had the same teacher. This year, I was certain we would have the same teacher, and wanted to be in the same class, at least that's what I thought.

"BECCA! You don't want to be in my class. You don't want the same teacher", Jullie said as her voice was rising.

"Of course I do, I never said I didn't, did I?", I said, trying hard not to attract attention.

"No, you didn't, but you said you didn't want to have the same teacher as me!", she answered.

"I want a different teacher, but I still want to be in your class", I spoke quietly.

"Sorry BEC, I won't yell again"

***

That was our first fight, and like I said, the one that started a trend.

Our favorite game in the summer was to act out scenes from Anne of Green Gables. After we watched the movie, we would each pick a scene and act out each one.

One day in mid-July, we had finished watching the movie and were ready to act out our parts. "Anne and Diana vowing to be best friends," I said. "Anne walking on the ridge pole of Muddy Sporrans kitchen roof," Jullie replied. We acted mine first and I was Anne because that was my favorite part. Then, when it was Julie's turn, she insisted on walking on the real roof.

"The roof is much more like the real thing!", she yelled. "The balance beam is safer," I yelled back. Then, Jullie stomped off down the street, her head held high. I ran inside looking just as silly as she had.

"What do you and Jullie want now?," asked my mother. "Julie doesn't want anything, she went home." "Why?" "We were acting and Jullie insisted that she had to walk on the roof because it was more like the movie!" I said she should walk on the balance beam, so she wouldn't get hurt. Then, she left. "We never used to fight, why are we fighting now?" I asked my Mom. "Disagreeing is making your friendship deepen." "What?", I asked. "When you and Jullie have your disagreements, you are learning stuff about each other and by learning these things you will be able to avoid them later." My mom turned back to her work and I left the room on my way to find something to do.

***

"...Jullie...," Mom said as she passed the phone to me. I was itching to tell her what I had learned, but I didn't have time. "BECCA!" ... "ya," I answered. "I broke my leg!" "How?", I asked. "Fell off of the roof!" "I'll be right over," I yelled as I slammed the phone back on its hook. One of the good things about our friendship was that we were always there for each other!

***

Dear Journal,

As I sat in my dorm reading a journal I had written in third grade. I wished that I had written about all of Jullie's and my good and bad times, even though we had had some "nasty disagreements," the good times had outnumbered the bad ones.

Yesterday I had a very unexpected visitor, I bet you could not guess who it was! It was Jullie! She stopped in on her way back to school after vacation. Seeing her brings back so many memories.

We discussed all our faults and strengths. Then, as if we hadn't had enough fun she brought out a photo album of us. We laughed till we would drop dead and tonight as the rain

152

comes down and I'm depressed about school, I can still see her happy face.

As she was leaving, she said to me, "BEC, you always bring out the best in me." I looked her straight in the eye and said, "ditto."

Love,
Rebecca King

Everyone Heidi connected with, in fact, did bring out the best in her and in them. Her brother, dad, classmates, aunts and uncles, cousins, me, her mom, the kids in the neighborhood and at Camp Calumet all brought out the good in each other and I believe this story was written with all of us in mind.

Yes, tonight, I read through this with my new understanding, gleaned from Heidi's message at my session with Maryann today. I finally hear her voice telling me that, though as parent-and-child, Heidi and I had many disagreements, and some of them "nasty," in the universal world, we are "forever friends." The vision I have is of her, dancing and skipping with her arms up in the air. "Finally," she says, as my tears flow and the love in my heart grows even more for myself and for our shared love through our continued communication.

That night in 1994, when Heidi insisted on finishing her story, I had no idea why this was so important and I now wonder if some unconscious, spiritual part of her knew something and this story was meant to be passed on to friends and people who were so important to her. It was her way of saying to all of us that she is still here for us. She is truly a "forever friend."

So, finish it, she did. And I am so glad that she did. The story is here for us all. I, her mother, had not included myself as a forever friend. Through my dear, gifted, intuitive Maryann B. Russell, I got the message loud and clear from Heidi that, yes, her brother, her dad, her friends, her cousins, her aunts and uncles, and then, the "WHACK!" that I was missing (I use the expression that "Heidi has to WHACK me over the head," because Heidi can't seem to get through to me without repeated messages). Me, me, ME! Her mom—forever. If you are one like me, who thinks this might be your child's message to others, think again and again. YOU FOREVER. As I write this tonight, chills are streaming through my body—beautiful, heartfelt, Heidi love and validation. After many years of rewrites of this section, I got it. Thank you, Heidi!

A precious part in Heidi's story also spoke strongly to me as her mother. Heidi portrayed Becca's fictional mom as a caring and wise mom. The advice Becca's mom gives about friendship and disagreements being opportunities for learning thus feels like a wonderful hug from Heidi through her story.

Heidi loved Anne of Green Gables with a passion. She identified with the characters in the story. Heidi too had a best friend. In fifth grade, they were starting to grow in different ways, still friends, but moving in their individual directions. Also, a third friend was becoming closer to Heidi, since during this time period they had more in common. The earlier best friend was someone who would take more risks than the other two. This story could easily have been a story about Lindsay, Rebecca, and many of Heidi's other friends. Her school friends, many years later, dedicated their high school yearbook to her—a tribute on their part to their forever friendship with Heidi). In Heidi's story, the presence of Becca's brother, whom Becca looks up to, is meaningful. Becca's brother, portrayed as older and wiser, embodies Heidi's love for her own brother. But, in real life, Heidi's brother struggled with survivor guilt when he was in college. At that time, Hans held himself as older, even though he was four years younger. For him, Heidi had remained an eleven-year-old, and he was now twenty-one, older than she ever got to be. They had had disagreements, as siblings do, and he held onto one of these quarrels as evidence that they did not get along. Of course, they had resolved that fight and her message, in her story, is saying to him that those disagreements did not matter. It was her way of saying to him, "I'm here forever and always."

For any of you out there, looking for messages, Heidi's story might help you believe that your loved one is there forever. Keep your eyes and hearts open for these messages—they are all around you.

Cindy Mitchell Perkins

Below are two poems by some of her forever friends, who wrote about her a few days after she died.

Heidi
by her friend, Lindsay

The way her face glimmered against her platinum blonde hair,
she was a ray of sunshine.
Her body was vibrant with color.
She would float around happily,
never finding the faults with people.
She would always climb through the faults,
to discover the good in people.
I can't say enough to express feelings for Heidi,
she was an amazing person that was always happy and spunky!
I hope that no one ever forgets what joy she brought to us!

Our Always Happy Friend
by her friends, Ellen and Kathleen

We will always remember your smiling face.
The way you laughed and talked.
1, 2, 3, 4, 5, 6, 7, 8;
which was your funny walk.

We never saw you sad or down
your face was never in a frown.
You were always there to comfort us,
whenever we would cry or fuss.

We never thought that we would part
but you'll always remain
inside our heart.

I found other messages in Heidi's room. When I finally had the courage to open her trumpet case, I found the music to two songs I did not know she had been learning to play. She had the music to "Amazing Grace," which she was to perform in church on "Youth Sunday," which was two days after her death. She also had the music to Eric Clapton's "Tears in Heaven." Coincidence? I think not.

Among Heidi's things, I also found drawings like the one shown.

A drawing found. . . drawn in the months before she died . . .

The bird so big . . . so alive . . .
The swing . . .so still . . .
So empty . . .
The sunflower so big and bright like her . . .
The tree . . . so strong and sturdy . . .
Showing no life . . .but still here.

What do all of these things mean? I really don't know for sure. I know they made me both profoundly sad and gave me great comfort over the years. Why?

As years have gone by, I have received other messages from Heidi in many different ways. They have kept coming so strongly that I have not been able in any way to deny them. Like the swing drawing, I found they often bring tears and smiles. Is the bird in the picture above connected to the eagles represented below?

Eagles
2013

On Eagle's Wings

Today, I learned what "On Eagle's Wings" truly means for me. Many folks I know cite an animal or a bird that they believe represents a lost loved one. For example, a cardinal may appear and a man know it is his mom. I was recently asked if I believe that an animal represents my daughter. I have seen orbs, and have photos of them. I know from a very deep emotional place that those have been Heidi visiting. I have seen rainbows that I have had such a strong emotional reaction to that I have been sure they were from her. I have sometimes seen animals and wondered if they were her, but never as strongly as the eagles I have seen recently. Many of the eagles I have seen on Swans Island, where I come to be close to Heidi, have flown by when my camera "just happened" to be aimed at a part of the sky where they flew.

This last week I came to my special Swans Island, off the coast of Maine, and spent an overnight preparing the camp for the arrival of my son and his new girlfriend. I had a joyous time, relaxing and visiting with the two of them. There is nothing like sharing in the joy of young love, especially when the glow of happiness shows as a giant smile on the face of your wonderful child.

As I left the Island, leaving the two of them behind for the weekend, I looked upward and asked Heidi if her brother and his new girlfriend were truly as happy as they appeared. After all, as a mom, I so want my children to be happy. I asked for a sign that would reassure this worry-wart mom. As the ferry went past the bell buoy that marks the arrival and departure to our island, I noticed a bird in the bell buoy. As we pulled on toward the mainland, I realized it was an eagle I had seen nestled into the top of the bell buoy. Tears rolled down and a very peaceful smile came to my face. I smiled all the way to the mainland and all the way home.

Today, I am back at the island for a longer visit. I went off for a paddle and found an eagle hovering around. I followed it around the bay for about an hour. I didn't want to leave it. Later in the day, I went off to the beach only to arrive at the parking lot to realize I had forgotten my carefully packed backpack. I turned the car around, retrieved my backpack, and, as I drove back toward the beach, the largest eagle I had ever seen flew very close alongside my car window, then landed on a low branch near the road. I pulled over, jumped out, and visited with the eagle for a while, as IT POSED FOR A SHORT PHOTO SESSION. Tonight, as I sat on the deck, relaxing, another eagle swooped into my view in the harbor and seemed to hover along my visual path to be sure we had connected.

This eagle-filled day reminded me of my paddle on Lake Ossipee, New Hampshire, earlier that summer. An eagle swooped by me as I paddled and then slowly worked its way to a point of land and settled on top of a tree. It seemed to want to be sure that I noticed before it landed in the tree. I did not have my camera, so I stayed nearby, watching, and visiting. I decided to stay until it flew off. A half hour later, I was starting to get cold, so I made some splashing noises thinking it would fly off. But finally I started to paddle back to camp, as the one who gave up first—much like in a staring game with a child and someone has to look away first. My newly found eagle friend had won that round.

Another time, after Heidi's friend had lost her twin babies well into her pregnancy, her friend's mom and I drove to the lake to visit with Heidi's friend and her husband and hold their grief with them. On the way, an extremely large eagle flew alongside our car long enough that we noticed and both had a strong reaction—tears in our eyes and our bodies shaking. A strong connection to that eagle was undeniable for both of us.

In summary, the answer to the question, "Do I have an animal that I know is my daughter stopping by for a visit?" is now a resounding YES. . . . .

On Eagle's Wings.

Orbs

The photograph on the cover of this book is one of many photos that I have taken over the years. It took me a long time to realize what orbs were and recognize Heidi in them. I had to allow myself to acknowledge the deep feelings that came when these appeared.

I had never heard of an orb until the fall of 2009, when they started showing up in my pictures as a small green ball, often looking like an eye, or even an entirely different shape. Heidi appears on the cover of this book, both in the clouds that look like her dancing in the sky and as the small green ball "orb" that I had come to recognize as her. This photo was taken along with many other photos on June 10th, 2016, at the time when she died in 1994, 22 years later. It took me years to notice the orbs in my photographs and realize that they were her.

In the fall of 2009, I had gone to a local campground on a beautiful full moon night for a few days' getaway. I camped right by the ocean. As the moon rose, I took many photos. I noticed that a small shining green ball had appeared in my photo. As I noticed it, I was brought to my knees and overcome with emotion. I sobbed as I sat on the ground, staring at the moon and the sky and the ocean that lay in front of me, knowing that Heidi was there somehow, someway, with me that night. My reaction emotionally and unconsciously was from my soul and not one I ever questioned. I just knew. I knew she was there with me in a way that I had not felt the strength of before. The depth of feeling I experienced left no question for me that this green ball was for me. Thus began our new way of communicating. As I like to remind myself of Heidi's persistence in communicating with me...

WHACK!

I stayed up most of the night that night taking photos and playing with the light that was my Heidi. I would focus the camera (an older SLR camera that did not let you see your picture until after you took it) where I thought she might be and see if she (in the form of the green orb) would be captured in the photo. I went that night from tears to laughter to tears of joy, knowing that I was in a new way playing with my daughter. I would guess where she would be and try to get the photo. I felt as if we were playing hide and seek together. I started to say, "OK, I think you are up there by that tree," and snapped a picture and looked to see if I had captured her in the form of this green ball. Many times, I got it right, other times I would laugh out loud, thinking "you got me." I didn't want to sleep, for I was uncertain whether I would ever have this kind of experience again. I have since had so many that I have lost count. What I did not understand at the time was that I had already taken many pictures that included an orb, but had not noticed them. I had thought they were just the result of bad lighting or something had been wrong with my camera. I went back over older photos and found her shining in many of them. I have had visits with my mom also in the form of beautiful orbs on Easter Sunday, at the sunrise service (something we had shared throughout her life). The Easter sunrise photo showed my mom as a bright yellow orb, which was different from Heidi's orb, and I had a feeling, like with Heidi, that mom was there and I should pay attention....

WHACK!

I uncovered more orbs in other pictures taken in a far-away land. Heidi's brother, Hans, had grown into a mature young man. He spent his junior year of college studying in Australia. There, he became tormented by the thought that he should have taken care of his sister. She was eleven when she died, and he was six. But she had remained eleven, while he had grown up. He was struggling, trying to figure out why he hadn't taken care of her. He had the strong image, inside him, of him being the big person he had grown into and her being the little eleven-year-old. I found that Heidi was holding her brother while he was there in Australia, battling his demons. There she was in his photos of Australia! That green ball was in several of his pictures from Australia....

WHACK!

??
??
???

I TOOK A BREAK AND CAME BACK TO FIND ALL THESE QUESTIONS MARKS ABOVE. Question marks that I had not typed in. (Another message from Heidi that I cannot explain, but know to be true.)....

WHACK!

I sit to write and there she is. Writing about her stirs up memories of "trumpet tripping," as I have come to call it—tripping over her trumpet each afternoon, as I came in the house. Heidi would drop the trumpet just inside our sliding glass doors and run off to her next exciting adventure. I would come home soon after and trip over the trumpet on my way in. In my frustration, I would remind her not to leave it there and take it to her room. What I would give to trip over that trumpet just one more time—the trumpet that I found with the music to Eric Clapton's "Tears from Heaven"!....

WHACK!

Two different friends with whom she had chatted about dying just shortly before she died....

WHACK!

An innocent look up into the sky to watch the clouds or the sunrise or the sunset and there is an angel in the clouds, right when I need comfort or strength. A tear drops down my cheek and I just know...

WHACK!

A strong comforting feeling washes over me when I am down, or scared, or feeling vulnerable—a feeling like someone is there, holding me, because someone is... there, holding me.

WHACK! seems like a funny word or sound to describe such a spiritual personal moment in time. Yet, for me it is absolutely the right word because I think that I, like so many of us, live in the world of proof

162

and concreteness. We have to see it, feel it. Research has to validate it or it is not true. I can't prove any of this to any of you. I just know for me it is true. You have to decide for yourself what is true for you.

I had to be "WHACKED" many times in order not to deny my reality and experience any more. I do not believe in coincidences anymore. I just smile now. Like so many, in the beginning, I did not want to share my stories, because I didn't want anyone to question them and expect proof from me. Some of my reluctance was rooted in my childhood experiences of my mother being made fun of for sharing just this kind of experience. I so wish mom and I could talk about that now. I believe she is smiling with Heidi and saying, "It's about time!"

I now know that I don't need proof… I know in my heart what is true for me and each person has to know what is true for them. And that is OK.

A dear friend who has lost a grandchild, and who has seen the orbs that I have seen, kept searching for proof. She kept being frustrated by people who did not believe her. She expected everyone to just go, "Wow! That's incredible!" But many people look for other explanations. The feeling inside your heart when you just know that orb is someone you love is not something you can prove or share in a way that is convincing for everyone. Often, when I share these stories with others, the response is "That's happened to me." If a communication from a dead loved one or something like that has reached you, you just know. These messages are my new way of communicating with Heidi.

HEIDI HUGS
by Mom

Heidi, my love
my heart aches without you here
my heart wants you to be here today
my arms are so empty
without you to hug
in the way I want to
the way we are used to
here . . . on earth
in our physical beings

You
send messages from above.
A friend asks
is there something in nature

Cindy Mitchell Perkins

some way she speaks to you
a cardinal
a butterfly
a dragonfly
a ???
YES . . . YES . . . YES
I want to yell
so much bigger
how do I explain?
So many ways
rainbows
letters
and the orbs

What's an orb?
You ask
I did not know
Now I do
A message from you!
A hug in a new way
so strong
so pure
so true
I dropped to the ground weak with emotion.
Shaking. . . . Tears. . . .
Sadness. . . . Joy. . . .
Smiles. . . .
That first night
when I saw and felt
your strong presence in the sky

and in my body
coming through my camera.

You are here!
the comfort
I receive from your universal arms
wrapped around me
indescribable
and yet
so warm
so very loving

The way I want it?
No

Comforting?
Yes

Both true
tears and smiles

THE HARD QUESTION
- How Many Children?

At first, after Heidi died, the question, "How many children do you have?", would often catch me off guard; tears would come before the words. My heart's answer is and was always two. The reply often leads to the natural questions: Their names? How old? What Grade? Boy? Girl? Now, many years later still: Where are they now? What are they doing? Grandchildren? All of these are seemingly innocent questions, with what should be easy answers, yet, life made these answers so much less easy.

I struggled, in the beginning especially, and now, some days, I still do. I tried all the answers. I tried, "I have two children." The well-intentioned questioners' response would then often be, "Oh, and how old?" My tears would then begin and often theirs too. Or I would say, "Hans is seven and Heidi died last year." The person who had asked would get quiet, or tell me how sorry they were. I would end up feeling as if I was somehow supposed to care for them. As if. . . .

I tried saying, "A son, Hans, seven," thus avoiding the pain in their eyes and the sympathetic "sorries," But, I felt empty inside when I replied that way. I felt that I had somehow betrayed Heidi—with this response of mine, it was as if she had never existed. It wasn't long before I realized that, in order to take care of my heart, I needed to speak my truth and say "Two: Heidi and Hans."

Gradually, I compiled different responses to this very emotional question. Some days, I was OK with this seemingly simple question, and the sympathy, and the tears welled up in both myself and those who had innocently asked. Other days, I learned to move the conversation on to their families, or change the subject very quickly before they had time to ask more. Sometimes, I would say, "My son, Hans, is seven," and go on to talk about him, thus managing to some degree where the exchange went. This would divert the conversation successfully, so, for that moment, I could choose not to share my whole story. I learned that how I answer, "How many children do you have?" was up to me and could be different on any given day. If you are faced with a question like this one, you too get to make that decision for yourself. There is no right answer.

Most of the time now, I say that I have two children, Hans and Heidi, that Hans is thirty something, doing whatever great thing he might be doing, and that Heidi died when she was eleven. I have learned most of the time to be ready for the other persons' sadness without needing to care for them. It took time to become comfortable with this answer, which I use more often than I had in early days. I am now very aware that I am opening a door and inviting the other person to respond to my loss, if they would like to. I have learned over the years that another person steps through this door I opened, often to express a loss of their own or of someone they know and we share our journeys. Often, there is comfort found for both of us in this sharing. There still are days when I don't open the door. Some days, this is just how I take care of myself, knowing that this is a day when I need to hold Heidi close to my heart and my grief private.

Hans Perkins Tobiason

I always want to celebrate my precious 6'2" blond-haired, blue-eyed baby boy, Hans. There is not a day that goes by that I am not thankful that he was spared. This recognition does not mean that it was better to lose one or the other. My wish is not to have lost either of my children. My wish is for you not to have lost any of your children. Which child died was not in my control.

The pain Hans has had to live with since June 10, 1994, is unimaginable. I cannot tell his story. He is the holder of his story. We all have our own personal experiences, including, of course, our children. As parents, we want to take away all pain and suffering from our children. We cannot. In the case of a surviving child or children, we cannot know the depth of their emotions around their experience.

I am painfully aware that I could have lost both my children that day. I am eternally grateful that I did not. His little boy's joy and sparkling blue eyes are why I got up in those early days. I wanted to be there for him. It wasn't until much later that I realized the burden that

I inadvertently imposed on him. I had relied on Hans emotionally as my reason for getting up in the morning. He also still carries now the load of being the surviving child.

I watched and held him in his pain. I marveled in his ability, like most children, to have his pain fully and then to move into the joys of his life with seeming ease. Observing this amazing coping strategy is where I got the expression that I so often use with parents who are hurting about their children: Children are like little Buddhas. They can be in the moment. They have their tears, anger, grief, and rage, then, they move on to the joys of their day. It is almost like a switch being flicked as we watch. We, the adults, can sit in our hard feelings for long periods of time. We hold onto them as if we don't have permission to have the good ones. We hang on tight. Children are very much capable of revisiting their pain. But they are just better at balancing both parts of their lives.

From Hans, I learned by watching him cry in pain as I held him and then look up and say, "can I go ride my bike?" or "can I go play with my friends now?" The answer of course was, "yes, yes, please do." Was his pain gone? Of course, not. Yet, he could move on to his enjoyment and happy self once he had had those feelings, more easily than most adults are able to do as they process their grief. It is also true that, as our children grow through different developmental stages of their lives, the questions and search for answers change as they navigate their way to hold their grief into and through adulthood.

He was and is a sensitive, soulful, and deep spiritual being. When he was 3, 4, 6, and on, he asked spiritual questions that seemed way beyond his years. Watching him grow into his mature soul has been a privilege. He has always been wise beyond his years and doesn't always recognize that—at least from my prejudiced mom point of view.

On a piece of paper, that I recently found, I had written down a conversation I had with young Hans about the day Heidi died. We had just returned from our vacation, so it likely was in 1995. My notes at the top of the page say that he had been easily tearing up over vacation. He wanted to visit with only one friend at a time, because he had a hard time dealing with more than one at once. He vocalized that he wanted to be with calm kids, not "wild" kids. While we were in the car that day, he had lots of questions (a car ride is so often when kids will have the hard conversations.) He wanted to know what lane we were in at the tollbooth. Then, he asked, "What did we hit?" He shared with me what he thought and his theories on how my arm and collarbone were broken. He talked about the cut on his head. Then, the questions began.

Hans: "Why didn't the driver try to turn and miss us?"
Me: "He did try, that's why he only hit one corner of the car where Heidi was."
Hans: Oh, then he would've hit Becca too. We would have been sadder.
Then he added: "I'm glad Becca is OK."
Me: "I'm glad YOU and Becca are OK."

Next hard question:

Hans: "Did Heidi die instantly?"
Me: "Yes."
And then I told him I knew that because there was a doctor in another car, who wrote us a letter to tell us that she tried to help Heidi and she had died right away.
Hans: "Yeah, I saw her and Heidi on someone's shirt."
My first inkling that my little boy had seen and remembered more details than I knew.
Pause
Hans: (almost a whisper) "She was so alive."
Me: "She still feels very alive to me."
Hans: (looking very relieved) "Yeah, I think she's in her room, or at school, or with her friends."
I talked about my counseling and that I was having a hard time with knowing she died and why she isn't in her room.
Hans: "Yeah, Mom."
I shared that I had talked about that with my counselor and how much that helped when she reminded me she is alive in our hearts and love.

Hans: "Yeah, she always will be, right?"
Me: "Yes."
Hans: "I guess I should talk about that with my counselor."
I asked if he meant like that feeling that it's hard sometimes to remember Heidi died but you really know she did.
Hans: "Yeah, cause you talk with your counselor about that, so, I guess I'll talk to mine about it next time."
Me: "OK, good plan."

We arrived home for bed time, He got mad at me and cried a lot. My note says everything normal again.

This conversation is a window into his world at such a young age. His little person was processing everything he had experienced. I was always thankful when he would voice his questions. One of my deepest and hardest pains is knowing that Hans, my little boy, had a clearer memory of the actual scene than I did. He safely told his story to his therapist and I heard from her and read his description in detail. I'm sure there was much more stirring around inside him than he was able to bring to the surface. His survivor guilt started the moment he lost his sister.

Survivor guilt is big and looming for our surviving children. Hans was younger than Heidi, yet, as he grew older, she stayed eleven and he went well past that. He became the older brother, who came to believe he should have taken care of her. This reality is in painful contrast with the way his life started with his adoring sister four years ahead, leading the way. They were a duo to be reckoned with.

During his junior year abroad, in college, he called me in the middle of his night, sobbing, as he got out the words, "it shoulda been me, mom. I was bigger, I should have protected her." This age mix-up is common for surviving siblings, because they continue to age and the child who has died stays the same age in their mind. We had a long conversation and he (for that moment) was finally able to hear that he was a little guy then, and there was nothing he could have done to save his sister. I wrote the following poem for him a few years later, as I witnessed him continuing to struggle after his return to the states.

Hans, Song of My Heart

IT SHOULDA BEEN ME
IT SHOULDA BEEN ME
THAT'S THE SONG YOU SING

As if . . . as if . . .
that would take away the pain, when you survived!!!
THANK GOD . . . THANK GOD . . . YOU SURVIVED
THANK GOD . . . THAT'S THE SONG I SING

My heart burns with pain for all you lost
that HORRIBLE day
the day your spark was covered up. . . .
It's still there just needing to be uncovered
I see it
sometimes you allow it to peek out

IT SHOULDA BEEN ME
IT SHOULDA BEEN ME
THAT'S THE SONG YOU SING

You lost your sister . . .
who loved you so . . .
the story you've written forgets sometimes . . .
thinking she's mad . . . thinking you were angry with her
NOT SO . . . NOT SO . . . I say to you

You both adored . . . loved . . . shared . . . enjoyed
(and yes sometimes fought and got angry—but not for long)
the short time you had together
you
were best friends to each other
the train ride to Florida

Cindy Mitchell Perkins

you hardly knew adults were there . . . 24 hours
you engaged in a world of two . . . laughing
creating . . . dreaming . . . playing

IT SHOULDA BEEN ME
IT SHOULDA BEEN ME
THAT'S THE SONG YOU SING

You lost your parents . . . to the depths of their grief
my bright-eyed little boy . . . I left to grieve so deeply . . .
your dad too . . . so buried by our grief . . . we weren't there for you as we
would have been and so wish we had

Your loss. . . . the worst . . . a little boy. . . . No playmate sister . . . to
create with . . .
parents often not emotionally available
all taken away in one fateful moment
your journey the hardest. . . . A small boy of six
cast into the world
SO ALONE . . . TO CREATE A STORY SO FAR FROM TRUE
a story that says

IT SHOULDA BEEN ME
IT SHOULDA BEEN ME
THAT'S THE SONG YOU SING

A story that dwelled on childhood memories that got rewritten
stuck in the place I your mom called out in terror to save your sister and
you thought
what about me?

IT SHOULDA BEEN ME
IT SHOULDA BEEN ME
THAT'S THE SONG YOU SING

Keeping Heidi Close

Your grief and isolation think that's what I, your mom said,
yet, NO NO NO
I so want you to hear
I KNEW . . .
for sure you would live
your eyes so . . . bright . . .to sing
your song so strong. . .
those eyes that pierce my heart
those soulful eyes
so strong and brave
eyes that heal and love

You have a gift of peace and healing
to be shared with others
you were doing that as such a young boy
it's still there . . . I know so deeply
you are doing it still

IT SHOULDA BEEN ME
IT SHOULDA BEEN ME
IT WASN'T ME!!!
Time for your new song to come forward

I, your mom, am so very thankful that
IT WASN'T YOU
IT WASN'T YOU
THANK GOD . . .THANK GOD
IT WASN'T YOU

YES . . . I wish it had not been the road we took
that our path had gone another way
that we had gone on to swim and sing into that summer and all those
years.
But
that was not to be

Cindy Mitchell Perkins

your sister gone
our song so quiet
our tears so many
your parents torn away from you when you needed us so much
so small . . . so bright . . . so alone

My heart so wants to go back and hold you tighter . . .
to have paid more attention to that beautiful soul that's you
that's not to be . . .
the song of the surviving sibling is the hardest and
yours
I wish I could take that pain for you.

I cried with joy . . . the day you were born.
A Boy. A Boy. Your dad kept saying
it's a boy. . . . He knew how I wanted you to be a boy. . .
Such joy. . . . You brought such joy
such strong soulful eyes

Look in the mirror and see what I saw that first moment
and see today
the joy . . . the intensity
the way you can look into someone's soul
in such a healing, knowing way.

IT SHOULDN'T HAVE BEEN YOU
IT WASN'T YOU

You have a gift to share
use your eyes and peacefulness to heal
to help . . . to lead . . . to create
to sing YOUR song

Your Gift
those soulful eyes. . . . Those peaceful, healing

BRIGHT BLUE EYES
THEY PIERCED MY HEART
THE DAY YOU CAME

THEY CALMED THE WORLD YOU WERE MEANT TO BE IN

So now my boy
my baby boy
my big strong man
look in the mirror and see those eyes
that others see so easily.
I am here, your mom, who loves you so,
to hold and hug and smile and love
and
remind you every day
IT WAS NOT YOU AND SHOULD NOT HAVE BEEN

LIVE ON WITH LOVE. . . HANS.. . . SONG OF MY HEART

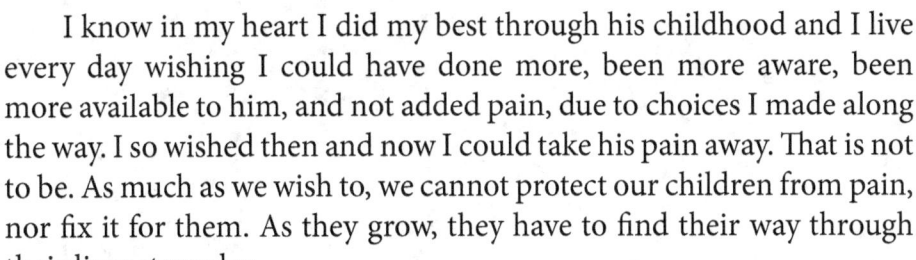

I know in my heart I did my best through his childhood and I live every day wishing I could have done more, been more aware, been more available to him, and not added pain, due to choices I made along the way. I so wished then and now I could take his pain away. That is not to be. As much as we wish to, we cannot protect our children from pain, nor fix it for them. As they grow, they have to find their way through their lives struggles.

Living with My Loss Through the Years

Helping Others Helps Me

It took me some time before I was able to offer support to other grieving parents. In the very beginning, I could not hear about anyone else's loss of a child. It was too big for me to hold my own loss, so the thought of someone else's was overwhelming. After a year or so, I was able to reach out and, when I did, I found that it helped me to sit with, talk to, or just show up for that other parent, like so many did for me in the beginning. I started to feel like I had something to offer someone else just by being me because I was in my life every day, albeit one step at a time. Because I know how much it meant to just see parents who are going on with their lives, I know that what helps is not the words, because there really are no "right" words, but it is showing up. I include below a series of journal entries that I wrote over the years, on occasions when I reached out to other parents I knew who had lost a child.

I Reached out to a friend tonight when I heard her son had committed suicide. A tragedy of our failed mental health system. A wonderful young man, a lost soul.

Now a mom who heard me say, . . . It's not supposed to happen this way. . ... . she replied from her quiet, scared almost a whisper voice. . . It's not the order of things.

No Friend . . . It is not.

* * * * *

Our family had also lost my nephew, when he was a young adult. Over the years, when we saw each other my brother-in-law Don and I would always hug deep hugs in our knowing way. We both believed we would see our children when we died. I went to see him when he was given two days to live. I asked him to say hi to Heidi when he saw her, assuming that that would be in a few short days. Everyone's prayers were answered for Don and he miraculously lived for two more years. In the course of those two years, he called one day and said he owed me an apology. I said, "whatever for?" He said, "well I haven't kept my end of the bargain," then laughed. I told him he could take his time with that bargain, there was no urgency. Our sense of humor, our faith, and our conviction that we would one day be reunited with our deceased child helped us both.

* * *

I drove to the home of one of Heidi's teachers, who had just lost his infant. As I got out of my car, the mom who had walked to my home many years before pulled in behind my car. We all hugged and cried. We both said that we're so sorry you are in this club. A club no one wants to be in and no one wants to greet their friend as they fall in with us.

* * *

To another parent, I said, "it just SUCKS." She said, "yes, yes it really SUCKS." I, like everyone else, asked if there is anything I could do. However, I knew as soon as I said it that there is nothing, short of bringing their beloved little child back, there is nothing. Nothing. I know that the profoundly sad and lost voice of another parent always takes me back to my first days and moments. . . . Feeling so helpless . . . so lost . . . so unsure. . . .

* * *

I sit with a long-time friend, a dad, his grown child lost ten years ago. Lost to a terrible disease. We share a campfire, a beach, a place filled with memories of our little girls. We don't always need to talk. We know there are no words that help. There really are not. We all try to say something. . . . Sometimes silence, a hug and shared tears are what you have to give and all that a parent can take in. Sometimes I say, "there are no words."

* * *

I called another parent a few years ago, who had lost her adult child. She said, "I got up this morning and went to work for part of the day because I need a purpose. I have to have something to get up for." I said, "I get that. If it got you out of bed and moving, if only for a little while, then it was the right choice for today. She said, "I would really like to get together. Maybe you could call, in a month or so. when I'm more able to have tea." I responded that I would like to have tea, if only so she can be with another mom. I said, "I will call before the week is over and offer a time. If you're not ready, that's OK, but I will keep offering." She sighed a relieved sigh, and said she would like that. By just being there, I hope to offer her some hope, as many moms did for me. She is putting one foot in front of the other, right now. I know that pain. I know that struggle. I know that strength. I know mine and I know those familiar pieces, but I don't know her pain. I only know mine. She is taking in what has happened and not able to have it be fully real yet, or maybe it is too real right now. If it's too much to comprehend today, hiding under the covers may be what feels right, or feels like the only choice. But this parent knew she had to try moving in another direction, so she went to work that day. Having a cup of tea seems like climbing Mount Everest today, yet she can imagine a time in the future when it will be what she wants. It will feel like that and, she will do it one moment, one step, one breath at a time.

***

Two friends who have lost a child and I get together regularly. We visit, talk about all the regular stuff, and sometimes we talk about our three children, all taken from us way before we planned. Not the order of things. We remember each other's anniversaries, we share when it's a hard day and why. We hold each other's pain, tears, and loss and we don't try to fix anything. We know.

***

Many of us will have tea, go for a walk, share stories about our children, share a campfire and will know it's not our words that help—it's just our being that does. Nothing magical, or special, or strong, or courageous. I am and they are parents carrying a hole in our hearts. Maybe knowing that I can and have gone on will assure another parent they too can climb this mountain. I know I will be reassured by others too when I need it. This reassurance will come in many forms. Sometimes, it will come when we walk together and realize the other has a quiet tear falling into their smile.. We will see a sudden rainbow and not need to say a thing, but just share a quiet knowledge that we are holding each other in our silence. I am feeling the weight of that mountain right now, as I think of all the other parents hiding under their covers tonight and waking tomorrow having to face another day, where the reality of their loss is overwhelming.

Maybe, reading this is what you need today. I hope in some way it helps you not feel alone. Be easy on yourself and let yourself do what you need in any given moment, as you walk this journey. Trust that what you are doing is right for you.

Other Losses in Our Lives

Other losses over the years will sometimes bring you right back to the moment of losing your child. The sense of grief is the same. You may find yourself at a service or hearing of another loss and suddenly feel yourself in your tightest grief. The actual loss is that of a different person or animal, yet the emotion will sometimes feel as hard.

I wrote this in 2019 after I lost my little Yorkie, Gus. I am two weeks into life without my dear Gus. He snuggled into my arms fifteen and a half years ago on Heidi's birthday. A week ago yesterday, my little four-pound buddy passed peacefully in my arms. His passing was another reminder to me of how death is not something to fear. He curled up in my arms, quietly and peacefully went to sleep, after his precious gift of fifteen and a half years with me. I realized, soon after, that he had been my companion longer than I had had Heidi here, with us. Something about this was sad and tearful, but also comforting and peaceful. Losing him has tightened that knot of grief that lives inside me always.

A friend said a few days later, "If only all of us humans could pass the way that Gus did." I replied, "That would be curled up in the arms of someone we love and just quietly going to sleep after a long and satisfying life." When we lose anyone—human or animal—we are reminded of all the losses we have had in our lives. The day-to-day adjustment of not having Gus here has brought back all the adjustments of missing Heidi and the intensity of the immediate loss. I keep thinking I need to check on him or take him out. I kept thinking I needed to get Heidi from school, or she was just in camp. He is just home, and I will see him when I get back. She was just off at a friend's house and would soon be home, or I should go get her. This reminds me of the conversation with Hans about how it felt like she was just in her room or somewhere else after she died. Gus's annoying bark is now something I long for. Heidi's trumpet left by the door to trip over was so quickly something missed and longed for.

In my 50s, I lost my mother and several dear friends. It seemed like these friends died one right after another. Every loss was very hard. I was privileged to sit beside several people as they took their last breaths. Being in the presence of someone dying or someone who has just died is an incredible honor.

Later when my dad died, I was in the room and stayed until they came to take his body. I walked in the room where my mother was still laying shortly after she died and in all these cases, I felt a peacefulness that was much like the sense of well-being I had felt when Heidi died. I knew all these people were OK. This is another one of those experiences that I can only tell you I knew. Such strong emotions go straight to your soul and heart. You just know and have no question. This is another layer of trusting. I feel blessed that I have had these experiences.

Knowing and believing that your person is at peace is not the same as also having your grief. I mentioned multiple truths before in this book and, indeed, this is a time in life where we are asked to hold two truths. I clung to the peacefulness and surety that Heidi was OK so strongly at first that, one day, my therapist suggested that maybe my trust and faith was getting in the way of my grieving. At first, my reaction was, "No, of course not." Over time, I realized that it was a way that I was keeping myself from feeling the depth of my pain and grief. When I could have that, I could also fully embrace my knowledge of "Heavenly Peace," as Wayne said in his Buffalo and Giraffe story.

Some people have said to me, "I won't get another pet because it is too hard to lose them." Others say they won't fall in love again, have another child or even get emotionally close to others because the loss is too hard. I believe, like so many others do, that the more you love, the harder the loss. I would not trade that deep love of my child, pet, parent, or friend for anything in this world. Yes, the loss of them in this world is so hard because we love so deeply. My lesson is that loving deeply is the only way to love. So yes, I will get another pet, I look forward to grandchildren, and hope to fall in love again fully and completely, knowing that the loss and grief are part of the deal. I have learned so much on my journey. Would I change that all to have my Heidi back? YES, YES, YES, but that is not to be. She is here in her new way, and I will continue to welcome her, grieve her, and learn from her. Thank you, Heidi, for all your gifts.

Where Am I Now,
Over Twenty-Nine Years Later?

My drawing by this sections title was done in a class just before Heidi's 40th birthday, in 2023. The picture describes where I am today. I am the bright light at the top of the mountain. I see and feel joyful energy around me and the grounding of this mountain that I have climbed. I have shone my bright light as I move forward in my life, embracing my seven decades here since my birth in 1952!

The poem "Fine Sand Beach," written in 1998, (on the next page) speaks to something that still happens when I visit Swans Island and this memory-filled beach. I take a little time to visit those memories and then, I also run, skip, and play, and rest on that beautiful beach, savoring the wonderful joy those memories represent. The last verse was added in 2023.

Fine Sand Beach

1998

The long Fine Sand Beach appears empty
not even a stone
so smooth
so empty

And . . .
so full
full of life
full of memories
full of a beautiful small blond child

Sleeping on a towel, under the umbrella
so as to be safe from the sun
so peaceful.

Toddling toward the water,
grasping the finger of mom and dad
so as to be safe from the big waves
so secure.

Laughing and running in a game of frisbee
growing with the cousins
so as to grow
in this island fantasy world
so safe.

Keeping Heidi Close

Singing the elephant song
holding the umbrella to be part of the story
gaining in self-confidence and creative expression
not wanting it to stop
so frozen in the moment.

Buried in the sand
only her blond, laughing head showing
so trusting of the others.

Dancing and reaching for the sun,
not afraid of being her own person
here on this special, safe beach.

And yet . . .
now the beach becomes
quiet again.
There is no blond child
who will come running to show me all the treasures she has collected this day.

My treasures for today
lay in the memories that this beach brings.
The long, smooth, fine, sand beach is empty today
no Stone
no Blond Child.

Yet, the memories bring the beach to life
in a way that stirs my soul
my smile comes through the tears
and I hunt for sand dollars
run into the water
and say thank you for
the memories
this beach is filled with love.

Today, like on so many days in my life, someone asked, "How many children do you have?" That question still goes right to my heart. That question is still hard. I know when I say two (which I do), they will follow up with more questions. How old? What are they doing? Grandkids? All the normal questions we all ask. I know that, when I say my daughter died when she was eleven, they will stop and catch their breath, tell me how sorry they are, tear up, not know what to say or tell me that their child has died too. Sometimes I cry as I say those words. Sometimes not. All those things still happen. All those things are OK with me. I expect them and am still very clear that my answer is two. I have two children. One lives here near me with his wife. I get to share my joy about him and be so proud of who he has become.

Today's exchange with a person who asked me how many children I have continued to a deep spiritual and life and death conversation. Finding kindred spirits or exploring life and death with people who are able to talk about that in a meaningful and honest way for us both offers continued healing. Those conversations inspire more thought and more questions. None of us has the answers.

More often lately, maybe because I'm not so young anymore, conversations turn to how we grieve, how we face our own mortality and what our perspectives are about life and death. I have my sadness, as I grieve the many losses we all go through as we get older. I am for the most part one of the oldest members of my family now. We are the elderly population. We are staring the end of our lives down now. What do I want to do with the rest of my life is always on my mind. Don't get me wrong, I'm very clear I plan to live to 120, strong and healthy. Really! It's not THAT unreasonable—my grandmother made it to 103!

I have had several conversations lately about how we live our lives as if we are never going to die. Maybe we have to pretend we are going to live forever in order to be in our lives. I don't feel old, I say. I'm only 70ish. I remember my aunt saying that same thing. She was in her 70's. I listened and thought how can you not feel old. She said her body reminded her, but in her head she was the same person. That made sense to me then. It makes even more sense now.

Because of my faith and the experiences shared in this book, I have no doubt that life continues on after death. I had a glimpse of that as I helped transition Heidi into the next part of her life. I am reassured and reminded of life's journey and my faith when I get the undeniable messages from her.

I say all the time, I do not know how people who do not have something to believe in, pick themselves up after they lose a child or someone they love deeply. My faith has gotten me along this far and I believe my Heidi has too. I want to be clear that I am not suggesting that you believe as I do. I just would suggest you find something to believe in that helps you move forward.

She is here walking with me in her new way that I have embraced and am so thankful that I have. I still have her. I still feel her presence and I still feel tears sliding down my cheeks as I think of her. I still want her physically here. I wonder what she would be doing and if I would have been holding her children in my arms or maybe her life would have been very different than my imagination can hold. Some days, I just want to hear her laugh.

This journey of grieving my child has been and still is a powerful paradox. I want her here and now AND I take immeasurable comfort in knowing still that she is OK and here in my life every day in this new way.

A dear friend and I had a conversation a few days ago at Camp Calumet, where I often have strong spiritual discussions. I was talking about my messages from Heidi and the many forms they have taken over the years. I was saying that I just know them to be true. He said, if we believe there is a God who created us, how can we not believe that such things and continued life in some other form is possible? Yes, Yes, Yes! Thank you, dear friend.

I am working, writing, running, kayaking, singing, and playing still. I am crying, grieving, hugging, holding on, and falling to my knees in grief still. I am reaching out to others. I like to think it's for them, yet I know some of it is also for me. Being able to offer some small piece of comfort to someone else gives me a kind of peace that I find nowhere else.

I go to services for friends and family to honor them. I go to support the people still here because I know how much it meant to me when people showed up. I grieve the loss of many friends. They, like Heidi, have lived their lives. I would choose for them to still be here also. Reality strikes us down many times during our lives. As I grow older, I lose more and more friends. I am watching friends live their lives with devastating news of illness or disability, yet they live. They are not dying! They are living. I hope that I will live all my life to its fullest as Heidi and so many of my friends and loved ones have.

I love that my son and his wife Kira are nearby and treasure their shared joy. Photos and talk of their adventures bring sunshine to my heart.

I pay attention to my new relationship with Heidi. I look to the sky for my little Orb-Angel. I smile when she shows up. I listen when she brings me a message in one of her many ways. I look forward to her visits and my connection with her. I will continue to keep Heidi close, as I continue on my life journey.

I hope that sharing how I have navigated these last thirty years is helpful to you in some small way. My hand is reaching out to you and I hope you see it, hold on to it, and feel the love and support. I hope that, by hearing my story, you will look a little harder, listen a little more closely for all the signs that say your child too is still with you. All of our children's loving souls surround us, support us, and walk with us every day. Embrace and trust what comes to you as you grieve.

Hug your friends and other family members. Hugs help. Caring smiles help. Music helps. Art helps. Conversations help. Writing helps. Meditation helps. Walking helps. Running helps. Old friends help. New friends help. Massages help. Loving helps. Strangers help. Books help. Throwing rocks helps. Drumming helps. Distraction helps. Poetry helps. Orbs help. Sharing helps. Believing in something helps. Faith helps. Holding onto your loved ones helps. Letting them hold you helps. Helping others helps. Trust that you will find your heart's path.

We love you all and hope in some small way our journey is a hand reached out that you can take hold of.

Cindy and Heidi

Resources

1. Bullens, Cidny, Somewhere Between Heaven and Earth, [album], Mommy's Geetar Music/BMI, 1999.
2. Cacciatore, J., Bearing the Unbearable, Wisdom, 2017
3. Eadie, Betty, Embraced by the Light, Gold Leaf Press, 1992.
4. Eger, Dr. Edith Eva , The Choice: Embrace the Possible, Scribner, 2017.
5. Flohr, C., Heaven's Child. Book Publishers Network, 2014.
6. Fox, Matthew, Original Blessing, TarcherPerigee, 2000.
7. https://www.bereavedparentsusa.org
8. http://www.calumet.org
9. https://www.cgcmaine.org
10. http://www.cindymitchellperkins.com
11. Https://www.compassionatefriends.org
12. http://www.maryannbrussell.com
13. Johnson, S., The Precious Present, Doubleday, 1984.
14. Leloup, Jean-Yves et al., The Gospel of Mary Magdalene, Inner Traditions, 2002.
15. Leloup, Jean-Yves, The Gospel of Thomas, Inner Traditions, 2005.
16. Melanie, B., Lifetimes, Bantam, 1983
17. Payton, Jeremy, The Gnostic Gospels Master Collection, Mindsparkpress LTD, 2023.
18. Perkins, Cindy, "Music, Rhythm, and the Safe and Sound Protocol," Theraplay® Innovations and Integration, edited by Hong, Rana and Coleman, A. Rand, Jessica Kingsley Publishers, 2023, pp175-185.
19. Peterson, Eugene H. (translator), The Bible in Contemporary Language, NavPress, 2005.
20. Stone, M., The Voice of an Angel, Marcy Stone, 2018.

Cindy Mitchell Perkins

GRATITUDE

My deepest gratitude goes to so many people for their support and blessings over the years and help to move forward with this book. My apologies to anyone I may inadvertently have left out. It would take another book to list each of you. I appreciate you all.

David, Best dad ever to Heidi and Hans, and Hans, Brother who turned out to be everything Heidi imagined as she waited for and celebrated his arrival. Thank you both for understanding the need to have this book published hoping it will be helpful and supportive to other families.

Abby Douglas for making sure she was buried next to a tree and who took me there in the pouring rain at midnight that first Christmas Eve.

Don and Abby Douglas for the solitude to do much of my writing and the final review of this book at their Belgrade Lakeside place.

Aunt Betty and Uncle Warren for their deck at Swans Island where most of the poetry was written.

John Tobiason for getting to us so quickly from Sweden.

Leslie Johnson for holding so many memories and tears with me.

Family and friends, each and every one of you who have supported us in ways that would fill a whole book over the years. You are the people who never forget, the ones who share a memory still and tear up with me at some of those times. You are the ones who know when a hug is needed and are available to just listen while I cry. Thank you for walking through this grief and pain with us.

All the parents and adults who rushed to the softball field in Yarmouth on June 10th to be with her friends and classmates as they found out what had happened.

The entire community of Yarmouth, Maine that has supported our family so strongly since 1994. Thank you for feeding us those first few months. Gail Daigle for organizing our meals and knowing the story behind Eric Claptons' "Tears In Heaven" , when I called sobbing the day I found the music in her trumpet case.

Mike Haggerty and Don L'Heureux, her beloved fifth grade teachers, who cared for her classmates so compassionately.

All of Hans' friends parents who kept him engaged with friends and little boy fun that first year and beyond.

Joan Wilbur who had the idea to dedicate the Softball field in her memory.

The girls who didn't know her who created Heidi's Hut at the softball field so the girls teams could sell snacks at their games. She would have loved that.

The entire Calumet community who held us together that first summer and still provide the place of comfort and support all these years later. Thank you for the Music and Drama building named in her honor that gives us a place to know she is remembered.

Dr. Stephanie Beukema for walking through my grief with me with such patience, caring, kindness, and skill over all those years of Therapy.

The Emergency Medical people who came to Exit 9 from several area communities on June 10, 1994. The Emergency staff at Maine Medical Center and Mercy Hospital.

All the people who stopped at the scene and tried to assist us. Thank you to those of you who took the time to write notes to us expressing your sorrow. Many of you were at the scene and many who never met us but, heard about us in the news.

Carolyn Carlson for staying with me that first night and being my arms that first week.

The school department of Yarmouth, Maine who made sure all the students were taken care of immediately after she died by providing grief counselors and made space available at the School for so many to gather and share their grief and memories.

My church community at First Parish Congregational Church, UCC in Yarmouth, Maine, starting with Lorraine Giles who provided pastoral counseling to me in the beginning up to the recent congregation whose accepting responses to my Peace Candle presentation about this book were the final push to get this published. This spiritual community has been my home base for 30 years.

The members of First Lutheran Church in Portland, Maine where we were members when Heidi died for the beautiful service and space for all who lovingly came to honor her life.

My Grad School classmates who held me up during our weekends of learning.

The Center for Grieving Children of Portland, Maine who provided support for many of Heidi's friends as they struggled with their grief.

Maryann B. Russell who has consistently and lovingly brought heartfelt, true and tender messages to me from Heidi. Keeping Heidi Close would not have been written the way it is without the gift of Maryann.

My writing group, Calliope: (Patricia Fuchs, Chris Chapman and Courtenay Snellings), who has listened to countless edits, shared memories and tears through many reorganizations and writings of Keeping Heidi Close. This includes the last minute editing help when I started to panic before sending something off for final approval. This groups continued presence and insistence that KHC has to get out there, kept me going many times when I could have stopped.

Bill Snellings whose photography skills made the inclusion of drawing journals possible.

Karetta Hubbard for the suggestion of the Keeping Heidi Close title which totally resonated and has stuck since the first suggestion.

Lynn Hjelmstad for your beautiful, loving design of the cover.

Florence Kilgo for your patience and care while providing the editing to this "new to the publishing world" person.

Robin Nelson, for jumping in and getting us to publication with such care and love.

Valerie Phillips for introducing me to Robin Nelson and Leaning-Rock Press.

All the parents who walked this path before me who shared their stories and gave me courage through their journeys.

Heidi for not giving up on our book and continuing to show me you are ever-present in our lives.

I love you all, Cindy

About the Authors

Cindy Mitchell Perkins, MA, LCPC lives in Maine with her dog, Luna. On June 10, 1994 her car was struck from behind instantly killing her 11-year-old daughter Heidi. Today Cindy maintains a private psycho-therapy practice, teaches Theraplay®, participates in running races, and spends as much time as she can with her friends and family. She loves to read, go camping, ride her bicycle, kayak and spend time with children. She finished her public school career in 2011 after being a teacher of most grades from pre-k through adult education and spending the second half of her school career as a school counselor. She has presented since the 1980's at professional conferences on topics varying from teaching math, using music and rhythm in therapy and employing various attachment and trauma interventions. She has run workshops on stress reduction, Zentangle®, creativity, and grief. In 2023 she published a chapter in a professional book, Theraplay®, Innovations and Integration Edited by Rana Hong and A. Rand Coleman. Her chapter, "Music, Rhythm, and the Safe and Sound Protocol in Theraplay," helps child and family therapists integrate these modalities. It is Cindy's hope that this book might offer a nugget of help to anyone out there who is grieving the death of a child or loved one. She can be reached www.cindymitchellperkins.com This is her first book.

Heidi Louise Tobiason lived her life in 11 years! She put full energy into those 11 years. There was nothing she tackled that was done with less than full commitment and drive. She continued on in that determined spirit in her new ways as described in this book. She loved her family and friends with her whole heart. She especially adored her brother, Hans. She talked and asked questions without time to take many breaths. Her spiritual presence is very much alive in this book as shown by her contributions. She was a friend to all and if you were her friend you were part of her family. I hope by reading this book you feel as if you have been added to her friend list as she would want you to be. This is her first book.

Final Note by the Author

This book is my open and heartfelt sharing of the pain, guilt, "if only's," hope, tears, journaling, letter writing, bargaining, therapy, spiritual struggles, and all that came with the death of my young daughter in the car that I was driving. I describe with openness and honesty the accident and the compendium of things I tried to help heal my heart after this unthinkable loss. My perspective today to say "yes, I am here, in my life!" speaks through the pages of this book. Yes, the pain is still in my heart. I have moved from those early days of not wanting to open my eyes to my new reality. I have learned how to hold my hurting soul, and I have gone on to have a wonderful, fulfilling life. I have changed and grown because of the loss of Heidi and the experiences that I was forced to have. I would change every bit of that to have Heidi back, but that is not to be. I offer up what helped me as suggestions for others. There is no road map. I am not in any way saying I know the answers. I do not. The book is an invitation into my experiences and into my heart and soul as I searched for new meanings and a way to learn to live with my pain and guilt. I share watching my young son struggle with the profound loss of his big sister and later, his survivor guilt as he became the "older brother," many years older than she ever got to be. I am reaching out to grieving parents and others experiencing profound loss so that maybe you might grab hold of something in my journey that gives you a piece of hope to grow from. I hope you will read this as if we are sitting together sharing as dear friends do.

With Love,
Cindy

www.ingramcontent.com/pod-product-compliance
Lightning Source LLC
Chambersburg PA
CBHW071325120626
46546CB00002B/444